1986

2-50

D1418734

© A. I. BOWMAN

ISBN 0 904966 08 9

Cover design by
Isaac McCaig, Kirkintilloch

Published by
STRATHKELVIN DISTRICT LIBRARIES & MUSEUMS
170 KIRKINTILLOCH ROAD, BISHOPBRIGGS, GLASGOW
Printed by
HOLMES McDOUGALL LTD.. GLASGOW

Kirkintilloch Shipbuilding

Background to Early Canal Shipbuilding

Shipbuilding at Kirkintilloch came at a relatively late stage in the development of the industry on the Forth and Clyde Canal. In the beginning, there was no building on the Canal; but the growth of Grangemouth as a port in the 1770s and 1780s and the steadily-increasing traffic on the Canal made it desirable to have some facilities at, or near, the entrance to the waterway. A small yard was set up at the Sea Lock by James Welsh. It is not known when it was started; but the earliest recorded building on the Canal is that of the sloop *Jean and Janet*, 47 tons, which he launched in 1782 for the Greenock shipowners, McAusland and Bog.[1] In the next year, he built the *Glasgow*, 50 tons, one of the first two track boats used by the Canal Company.[2] The other, the *Lady Charlotte*, was built at the Canal Basin, Hamiltonhill, by Archibald Munn, of the Broomielaw firm of J. & A. Munn.[3] Building by James Welsh has not been traced beyond 1788.

In the decade of the 1790s, the Canal Company provided carpenters' yards for boat-building and overhauling at Tophill, on the outskirts of Falkirk, between Locks 9 and 10; at Hamiltonhill, in the Canal Basin; at Kelvin Dock, Maryhill, between Locks 21 and 22; and at Bowling, in the basin at the western Sea Lock.[4] At Tophill, Kelvin Dock and Bowling dry docks were included in the yards. At Hamiltonhill, there was a small slip dock. These yards were primarily for the building and maintenance of the Canal Company's vessels. At Tophill, the yard was used for no other purpose, except for making and repairing lock gates; but at the other yards, building and overhauling for owners other than the Canal Company was permitted and even encouraged, as a source of income.

These yards were equipped for the building of wooden vessels to the dimensions dictated by the locks on the Canal, which were 70 feet long and 20 feet broad. The main types of craft built were lighters and scows; but sloops, gabbarts, ketches, small brigs and schooners were turned out at Bowling and Kelvin Dock, as well as drawn vessels.

A new stage was reached with the appointment of Thomas Wilson as Resident Engineer at Tophill in 1822. Wilson had made a name for himself a few years earlier when he built the passage boat, *Vulcan*, at Faskine, on the Monkland Canal. The *Vulcan* was an iron vessel, the first in Scotland. She took up station on the Forth and Clyde Canal in 1819, running between Port Dundas and Lock 16.

When Wilson came to Tophill, he adapted the yard for iron work and started to build iron scows and lighters. In 1829, the Canal Company decided that, in future, all its vessels should have iron hulls.[5] One reason for the adoption of this policy was the development of the coal trade on the Canal following the completion of the Monkland & Kirkintilloch Railway. Kirkintilloch was already a port of call for passage boats and other vessels trading on the Canal. As a terminus of the railway, it assumed a new importance for the Canal trade; but this was as a loading port rather than a port providing building and overhauling facilities. At this time, the main industries of the town and its vicinity were connected with weaving and spinning, or with agriculture. Its importance in the movement of coal was recognised in the construction of the Railway Basin at the Canal in 1834-35.

Kirkintilloch was not involved in any of the early experiments with paddle-steamers on the Canal, from Symington's two stern-wheelers between 1801 and 1803, up to Kibble's *Firefly*, with its endless belts of floats running over side paddles, which ran on the Canal between 1845 and 1849. Consequently, it was not affected by the impetus to shipbuilding on the Canal which came with these experiments. At the mid-point of the 19th century, shipbuilding and overhauling facilities on the Canal were grouped round Glasgow at the west end and Falkirk at the east end. In the long stretch of the Canal at its top level between Lock 20 at Wyndford and Stockingfield on the north of Glasgow, there was no yard where vessels could be drawn up for repairs and overhauling or where new craft could be built. Kirkintilloch, situated about the middle of this stretch, was a busy port, heavily involved in the timber and coal trades and in the development of its own new industries of calico printing, iron founding and coal mining, all of which required transport facilities on the Canal. An enterprising farmer, William Hay of Hillhead, had seen the possibilities in this sphere and, with his son, James, was building up a considerable Canal transport business with a fleet of scows. The lack of a local yard for overhauling and repairing his vessels was a considerable inconvenience.

In 1856 occurred an event of considerable importance to Canal shipping. James Milne, the Canal Company's engineer at Hamiltonhill, tried the experiment of converting one of the Company's iron lighters, the *Thomas*, to screw propulsion. The experiment was a complete success and supplied a satisfactory answer to the problems of steam engines driving canal craft — an answer which had not been provided by the paddle-steamers. In the next few years, many horse-drawn lighters and scows were converted in the same way as the *Thomas*, and steam lighters were being built at Kelvin Dock, Blackhill and Port Downie. The *Glasgow*, built and engined by David Swan and his brothers, John and Robert, in 1857, at Kelvin Dock, was the first of these. She is generally considered the progenitor of the "puffer".

In 1857, the year of the *Glasgow's* building, James Hay set up business at Port Dundas as a shipping agent. He must have been interested in the development of these new steam-driven lighters. His two younger brothers, Robert and John, were engineers. It is likely that the Hays converted some of their iron scows to steam propulsion. This, at any rate, is the local tradition, although it is not clearly supported by definite evidence. Such a development in the Hay fleet would make it more desirable than ever that they should have their own facilities for repairing and overhauling. They had an engineering shop adjacent to their premises at Midwharf, Port Dundas, where they could make and assemble engines; but they had nowhere for docking or slipping their vessels.

In the late 1850s and early 1860s, there was an unemployment problem in Kirkintilloch owing to the introduction of machinery in the weaving and spinning industries. A Working Men's Association was formed with the object of helping the workers to improve their lot. Although most of its activities consisted of uplifting lectures on such abstruse subjects as "Ancient Nineveh", delivered by well-meaning clergymen, it did give some consideration to the problems of self-help and co-operative working. One of the ideas which was beginning to be promulgated in Scotland at the time was that of the shipyard run on co-operative lines. Kirkintilloch must have been one of the first places in Scotland to take up the idea, which served the double purpose of providing a much-needed facility for local scows and lighters and also of giving employment to local men. The venture, styled "Crawford & Co.", developed into an industry which played an important part in the life of Kirkintilloch for almost a century and made significant contributions in its field. The boat-building yard started in the mid-1860s became a notable factor in the town's industrial life. As a co-operative company, it had a short life; but it was taken over by James Hay and his brother, John, and they built it up at a time when shipbuilding on the Canal had left an earlier stage of experimentation and was developing as an industry geared to the current requirements of Canal trade by steam vessels. The Hay brothers, with their yard at Kirkintilloch, and their engineering works at Port Dundas, played a noteworthy part in this development — so much so that the Kirkintilloch yard continued to function long after all the other yards had closed down. By contrast, the other Kirkintilloch shipbuilding firm, Peter McGregor & Sons, came into being much later and covered only a short span of two decades at the beginning of the 20th century; but in that time, it acquired a good name and enhanced the reputation of Kirkintilloch shipbuilding established and maintained by the Hays. Between them, the two firms made the industry an important feature of Kirkintilloch as Scotland's most inland shipbuilding centre, and did so on consistently amicable terms which prevented any competitive ill-feeling and allowed each firm to complement the other in promoting the general welfare and reputation of the town.

Crawford & Co. (1866-1867)

The origins of the co-operative company which started a boat-building yard at Kirkintilloch are obscure. There was a certain amount of boat-owning in the Kirkintilloch area. The Hays were perhaps the most prominent; but coal masters James Gardner of Meiklehill and James Duncan of Auchinairn had craft on the Canal, as had Thomas Whitelaw of Kirkintilloch and Matthew Hay of Kilsyth. The Hornes, Winnings, Gartshores and Nielands had boats trading from Kirkintilloch. It is probable that the founders of the company counted on, and may have obtained, support from these persons. There is some reason to believe that Matthew Hay Muirhead, a lime merchant, and his brother, William, a wine merchant and public house owner, had an interest in the venture. They certainly appeared at launches as guests. Archibald Stewart, too, of the Waterloo Inn at Hillhead, seems to have had some connection with the yard. His inn was a favourite haunt of puffermen and scowsmen. It is not unlikely that many of these individuals had a financial interest in the company. The company took its name from Samuel Crawford, who is thought to have been a connection of the Hay family. He is referred to in the obituary notice of Mr John Hay in the *Kirkintilloch Herald* of 25th August, 1915:

> Almost half a century ago (48 years ago, to be correct) boat-building had been started in Kirkintilloch by the late Mr John Thom, and Mr Crawford, both of whom had had experience in the work on the Clyde. They carried on for three years when Mr Hay and his brother took over the business and, under Mr Thom's supervision, and largely to his design, boat after boat of the steam screw-type were built. . . . .

Samuel Crawford's later career indicates a man of considerable ability both in shipbuilding and in community affairs.[6] John Thom worked at the yard for the rest of his life. His early training on the Clyde obtained a fine outlet in the work he did at Kirkintilloch.

Samuel Crawford started the yard in the autumn of 1866, with John Thom as his Foreman. It was located on the south bank of the Canal, just west of the Townhead Bridge. The keel of the first vessel was laid in October. She was launched on 23rd March, 1867. The *Glasgow Herald* of Saturday, 30th March, 1867, under the heading "Kirkintilloch: New Boatbuilding Yard" reported:

> On Saturday last, about 1 o'clock p.m., the waters of the Forth and Clyde Canal near Kirkintilloch were unusually disturbed and the people of the town greatly interested by the launching of a small craft from the newly-established boatbuilding yard of Messrs Crawford & Co. This young firm, the partners of which are already highly spoken of in the neighbourhood, began operations about six months ago on the southern bank of the Canal, immediately to the west of the drawbridge at the Cowgate. The first result of their labours is a composite lighter, about 100 tons burthen: 62ft in length, breadth 16½ft, depth 8ft. It is to be employed in the coasting trade and is the property of Messrs Colthorpe & Dewar, Dumbarton. The novelty of the thing brought crowds of people from all quarters of the town to the spot to see the launch, the ceremonial part of which was performed by Miss Muirhead of the Saracen Inn. Mr James Stark, a gentleman well known in the neighbourhood, at the request of the firm, assisted the workmen, and the decision and skill which he brought into play on the occasion contributed not a little, we are informed, to the final success. Miss Muirhead broke a bottle of wine in the usual way on the head of the devoted lighter, and wished success to the "Rainbow" which, thereafter, softly and quickly left the land amid the cheers of the delighted spectators.

The *Oban Times* of the same date stated that the launch was done broadside on and expressed the hope that the builders would "continue to turn out vessels from time to time". This hope does not seem to have been immediately realised. The *Dumbarton Herald* of 18th June, 1867, had the following report from its Kirkintilloch correspondent:

Our little boat-building concern is kept busy with repairs, but it seems there is no new work offering. This little co-operative venture should succeed, for the men seem very able for their work and not afraid of it.

There is no evidence that Crawford & Co. built any other vessel. A local tradition that an iron lighter called *Ceres* was built at the yard in 1865 seems doubtful. The date is almost certainly wrong.[7] The statement of the *Kirkintilloch Herald* of 25th August, 1915, that Crawford and Thom had the yard for three years is open to question. By the autumn of 1867, it seems to have passed to the Hays. An entry in the Canal Company's record of water taken from the Canal states:

7th October, 1867 — J. & J. Hay, Kirkintilloch — Slip Dock.

A note beside this entry reads as follows:

The Slip was occupied by Mr Samuel Crawford for a short time before M/s Hay. There is not any record in Canal Books of applications having been made or sanction given to take water from the Canal, to either party.[8]

If J. & J. Hay had the slip dock by October, 1867, then Crawford & Co. cannot have been in occupation for more than a year. Just what is meant by "slip dock" in this context is not clear. It usually implies an inlet on the bank with a slipway at the landward end. Such a slip dock was later constructed with the approval of the Canal Proprietors. It involved water being taken from the Canal to float the vessels up to the slipway, where they were hauled ashore. It is possible that Crawford & Co. dug a small inlet at the west end of the yard, without lining it with masonry or wood. The Canal Company had such an inlet at Tophill. It has been suggested that the Canal water was taken for the boiler of a steam engine used to haul up vessels on the slipway; but when water was taken for this purpose elsewhere, the Canal records state so explicitly. Certainly, the west end of the yard had a slipway from very early times, where scows and, possibly, smaller screws were hauled up. The Canal Company's map of 1867 shows the yard on the south bank west of the Townhead Bridge, with a group of three buildings in the centre of it, but with no indication of a slip dock or of a building berth. Canal maps, however, frequently left out such details. No permission for the construction and use of a dock in connection with the slip seems to have been given at this stage, and it must be assumed that, if there was one, it was filled in or allowed to fall into disuse. There is no record of a steam engine having been used to winch up the vessels using the slip. In the time of the Hays, a hand winch was used, and it is likely that hand winching was done in the time of Crawford & Co. No other information about the yard, its plant and equipment has been found. The fact that the *Rainbow* was a composite vessel — that is, had an iron frame with a wooden hull and decking built onto it — indicates that the yard was able to do some iron work as well as woodwork. As the *Rainbow* was launched broadside on, there must have been a building berth separate from the slip. When the Hays took over, they used a berth at the east end of the yard. It is likely that this was used by Crawford & Co. also. Samuel

Early view of the slip at the west end of Hays' boatyard. The vessel is said to be the *Charlotte*, one of the original Canal Company passage boats of 1809, converted into a lighter in the late 1830s.

Crawford and John Thom are the only names found so far of persons who worked at the yard. The *Glasgow Herald* speaks of the partners of "this young firm"; presumably it is referring to them. There is no indication that employees of the Company had any share in it financially; but if the later practice in the Hays' Company is any guide, it is possible that some of them had, possibly on a co-operative basis.

So far, no indication has been found as to why Samuel Crawford left the business in 1867 when the Hays took it over. Possibly the lack of orders put him into financial difficulty and his relatives came to his assistance. He went back to the Clyde, where he made a name for himself as Yard Manager with J. & G. Thomson of Clydebank. John Thom stayed on at the yard as Foreman Carpenter.

J. & J. Hay (1867-1896)

When the Hay brothers, James and John, took over the boatbuilding yard at Kirkintilloch in 1867, they were already well established as shipping agents and traders on the Canal. Their father, William (b. 1795) was a farmer at Hillhead who started boat-owning in the 1830s or 1840s and used his vessels for trading on the Canal. Voters' Lists and Census Records for Kirkintilloch show him abandoning farming for boat-owning in the 1840s and reverting to farming in the 1860s.[9] James Hay, his eldest son, was involved in the boat-owning business from about 1850 and, by 1857, had set up business at Port Dundas as a shipping and forwarding agent and was living in Glasgow.[10] This was the year after James Milne's experiment with fitting the *Thomas* for screw propulsion. James Hay's younger brothers, Robert and John, were engineers. According to family and other tradition, they tried their hand at engining some of William and James' scows. There is no definite evidence of this; but James' business was prospering and, in 1862, he was able to take delivery of the iron screw lighter, *Alice,* launched for him by Robert Wilson at his Port Downie yard.[11] William Hay had left the business by this time; probably his son, John, was involved in it, although in what capacity is not clear.[12] In 1863, James Hay had another iron screw lighter, *Alfred,* 51 gross tons, built by J. & R. Swan at Blackhill. She was fitted with a 2-cylinder, direct-acting diagonal engine of 12hp by J. & J. Hay at Glasgow in 1863.[13] This indicates that James and John were working together on the engineering side. According to the Post Office Directories of Glasgow, John Hay took up residence in the city in 1867. By that time, the Hay fleet of screws had been augmented by the *Albert,* 52 gross tons, and the *Victoria,* 54 gross tons, built at Kelvin Dock in 1865 and 1866, respectively, and by the *Adelaide,* 72 gross tons, built by Murray at Port Glasgow in 1866. The size of these vessels is an indication of James Hay's interest in the coasting trade. In 1869, he started a line of coasting steamers with the *Palermo,* 251 gross tons, purchased from Mories, Munro & Co. Before this, however, he and his brother, John, formalised the existing informal arrangement for working together in the Canal business by a written partnership agreement, entered into in 1867, in which the terms of the partnership and the division of responsibility between the brothers were clearly outlined.[14] In it, John Hay is referred to as "Manager", indicating that he had already been working with his brother, James, in this capacity. In the agreement, he became junior partner. The firm was styled J. & J. Hay.

When J. & J. Hay took over Crawford & Co.'s boatyard at Kirkintilloch in 1867, they intended to use it for a somewhat different purpose from that for which it had been started. Crawford & Co. had hoped to make it a building yard; the Hays regarded it as a place for maintenance and repair of their Canal vessels. They had at least five steam screw lighters and a fair number of horse-drawn barges and scows. Although they had an engineering shop and some wharfage at Port Dundas, there were no facilities for slipping vessels in the area which they occupied at Midwharf. The Canal Company's slip dock at the Old Basin, Hamiltonhill, was not readily available and was expensive. It was obviously to the advantage of J. & J. Hay to have their own yard; and

Yours truly James Hay

Kirkintilloch, with which they were so closely connected, was both suitable and less expensive. In the partnership agreement, John Hay had charge of plant and personnel, while James looked after finance and freighting. John's contacts at Kirkintilloch during his time as Manager to James were, doubtless, an asset in establishing the yard on its new basis.

From the outset, the policy of the Hays was to use the yard primarily for the repairing and maintenance of their own vessels. This policy was maintained throughout their tenure of the yard. It was both convenient and economical to be able to slip their canal craft in their own premises and in their own time, rather than to send them to Port Downie in the east or Kelvin Dock or Blackhill in the west, where they would have to take their turn with other vessels. In the event, as the Hay fleet grew in size, the facilities of these yards had to be brought in from time to time, to deal with overflows in the work schedule. The policy of keeping the yard to themselves was probably also influenced to some extent by the aim of the partnership to secure a monopoly, as far as possible, in the Canal traffic. As far as building was concerned, the Hays made it a subsidiary activity, to keep the work force at the yard occupied when there was a lull in repair and maintenance work. With only a few exceptions, all the vessels built at the yard were for the Company. It did not seek outside orders. In the earlier stages of the yard, building was experimental. The Hays were interested in evolving suitable types of canal lighter and coasting boat to meet the various trading requirements — carriage of timber, coal, sand and pig iron on the Canal; barley for distilleries and some coal for the coasting trade; and miscellaneous cargoes picked up in the course of general trading. John Hay had his own ideas about what he wanted in the way of Canal vessels and in John Thom he had a foreman who could translate them into practice. As the yard grew in experience, it was able to take on another building activity, buying up wrecked or disabled steam lighters cheaply, putting them into good working condition and either selling them profitably or using them as replacements of vessels wrecked or sold. The yard developed its own salvage squad, which was able to travel to wrecks or stranded vessels and patch them up for transit to Kirkintilloch.

For about 18 months from the time they took over the yard, there is no record of the Hays building any vessel there. Presumably they were occupied with maintenance of their craft and bringing the equipment of the yard into line with their requirements. In 1869 they built their first vessel, launched in May of that year. The *Lennox Herald* of Saturday, 15th May 1869, reported as follows:

> On Friday a small screw steamer of 90 tons, intended for the canal and coasting traffic, was launched from Messrs J & J Hays' yard. After being named the Helena, by Miss Jeanie Muirhead, the steamer glided broadside on into the Forth and Clyde Canal.

Miss Jeanie Muirhead is thought to have been a daughter of Matthew Hay Muirhead, a local lime merchant and a cousin of James and John Hay. Little is known of the *Helena*. She is believed to have been named after William Hay's first wife. As she was used in coasting trade, she must have had hatch coamings

James Hay (1829-1879).

Photo courtesy J. M. Hay.

and covers and a mast and a winch for working her derrick. Her gross tonnage was 42. Her dimensions — 64.3ft. × 14.45ft. × 5.7ft. — made her somewhat smaller than the other steam screws. She had a single-cylinder engine of 10hp, built and fitted, along with her boiler, by J. & J. Hay at Port Dundas. She had a short life, being lost off Davaar Island, at the entrance to Campbeltown Loch, on 23rd July 1877.[15] No further building at the yard is recorded until 1872; but in 1870 J. & J. Hay took delivery of the *Louise,* an iron screw lighter very similar in tonnage and dimensions to the *Helena.* She was built by David Swan at Kelvin Dock, but was engined by J. & J. Hay with a 2-cylinder high pressure direct acting engine of 15hp — an advance on the *Helena's* single cylinder 10hp engine. It is likely that John Hay and John Thom compared the performances of the two vessels with a view to developing a better design. The *Louise* worked for the firm until she foundered off Craigmore, Bute, on 3rd February 1893.[16]

The next vessel to be built at the yard was an iron lighter. Her launch was reported in the *Dumbarton Herald* of Thursday, 15th August 1872:

> On Tuesday afternoon there was launched from the boatbuilding yard here of Messrs J & J Hay, shippers, Port Dundas, a handsome iron lighter, of 85 tons burden. This is the second vessel built at Kirkintilloch by the Messrs Hay, who designed this lighter for their own carrying trade on the canal. Before gliding into the canal, the vessel was gracefully named the Hugh of Glasgow, by Miss Stewart, of Waterloo Inn. Many of the townspeople were present.

Miss Stewart was a daughter of Archibald Stewart, proprietor of the Waterloo Inn at Hillhead. In his early days he had eloped with one of the daughters of William Hay. The Hay family had disapproved of one of their girls marrying a publican. There seems to have been a reconcilation. The Inn was much used by crews of the Hays' lighters. Archibald Stewart's daughter Susan had a small grocer's shop attached to the Inn, where the lightermen and scowsmen could obtain groceries as part of their wages. A notice in the shop disclaimed any responsibility under the Truck Act. It is believed that the Hays gave the shop some financial backing.

The newspaper's remark, that the Hays designed the lighter for their own carrying trade on the Canal, is a pointer to the experimentation in types of vessel suitable for the trade being carried on. As the work of the yard progressed, the requirements of the firm as shippers were wedded to their experience as builders and eventually produced distinctive types of screw lighters which served their purpose very well. An interesting limitation on building was contained in an Agreement of 1867 between the Caledonian Railway Company and the Forth and Clyde Navigation, parties of the first part, and the Traders on the Canal and others, parties of the second part (including James Hay). Item 3 of the Agreement stated that:

> . . . those of the Traders who are at present owners of screw steamers on the said Canal shall be entitled to continue to use screw steamers on the said Canals, provided that size and construction of such steamers shall not be altered except with the consent of the first parties.[17]

In view of the limitation imposed by the size of the Canal locks the provision about the size and construction of steamers on the Canal would seem unnecessary. As far as the Hays were concerned the provision was of no consequence, as their designs were confined to only a few types, all governed by the requirements of Canal operation. What they were looking for was boats which could combine canal working with estuarial and coastal trading. Steam screws for Canal work only were fairly straightforward, being simply a development of the horse-drawn lighter with an engine put in it. They had no mast and had open holds, without coamings and covers. Apart from some of their earliest conversions, the Hays showed little interest in this type of lighter. From the time of the *Helena* they were looking for a type with a wider range. They must have learned something from the various builders who supplied them with screw lighters — Robert Wilson at Port Downie with the *Alice*; the Swan brothers at Blackhill with the *Alfred* and at Kelvin Dock with the *Albert* and the *Victoria*; Murray at Port Glasgow with the *Adelaide*. In the decade of the '70s and for some years thereafter John Hay and John Thom were experimenting on the basis of what they had learned, and also, perhaps, with the advice of Gilbert Wilkie, who had taken over the Port Downie yard from Robert Wilson and who seems to have had a close connection with J. & J. Hay.

Two more vessels followed the *Hugh* — probably lighters of the same type. Then came a more ambitious effort in an iron screw lighter for the coal trade. She was a departure from the Hays' policy, in that she was built for James Gardner, a coal master whose colliery was adjacent to the Hays' lands at Hillhead. There was probably a neighbourly element in this job. The launch was reported in the Kirkintilloch column of the *Dumbarton Herald* of 6th November 1873:

> On Friday there was launched from the boat building yard here of Messrs. J & J Hay, ship agents, Glasgow, a fine iron lighter of 120 tons. It was gracefully named by Miss Gardner "The Eliza of Kirkintilloch", and when completed with engines etc. will be ultimately employed in the coal trade of the district by Messrs. Jas. Gardiner & Sons, coal owners. This is the fifth vessel of the kind turned out by this firm since they came here.

The vessel was much larger than any so far built at the yard. Although apparently christened *Eliza*, she was registered as *Lizzie Gardner*, an iron screw lighter of 75 gross tons with dimensions 65.8ft. × 18.6ft. × 8.6ft. Presumably she was built to her owners' specifications and design, although it would be reasonable to assume that much of the detail was left to John Hay and John Thom. Her 2-cylinder 20hp engine was supplied by the Canal Basin Foundry Co.;[18] so that consultation on the engineering side must have been required. The *Lizzie Gardner* worked for the coal company until she was wrecked on 30th January 1881. She was an important ship for the yard, giving John Hay and John Thom valuable experience. The design capacity at Kirkintilloch, in the way of drawing office facilities and technical qualifications among the staff, appears to have been limited. The *Lizzie Gardner* gave John Hay and John

Thom a basic design on which to exercise their undoubted talent for improvements and modifications. The experiments over the next few years, however, show that they were feeling their way forward and had some distance to go before they arrived at the types they were seeking. The next building after the *Lizzie Gardner* was the *Leopold*, launched in 1875. She was a small iron screw lighter of only 35 gross tons. She had a single-cylinder 10hp engine by J. & J. Hay. Her dimensions — 66ft. × 13.2ft. × 4.8ft. — allowed her to enter the Monkland Canal through the Blackhill Locks. She must have been primarily intended for the Canal trade; but the fact that she was fitted with a mast suggests that, like the *Helena*, she might have been meant to go further afield on occasion. This is confirmed by a photograph of her taken at Oban, which shows her with bulwarks fitted. Bulwarks were usually dispensed with in craft working solely in the Canal, as this facilitated working the locks and loading and unloading. The *Leopold* was perhaps an early prototype of the smaller boats of the early 20th century, which did much of their work on Canal running only, but which were designed for estuarial work also. After just over twenty years with the Company she was sold, on 7th January 1896, to the Carrying & Transport Co., Goole. She was still afloat in 1935.[19] Her influence can be traced in the *Beatrice* and *Alice* (2), both built at the yard in 1888 and having dimensions similar to those of the *Leopold*, except for a slightly deeper hold and a slightly larger gross tonnage.[20] It was further continued in a modified form in three small iron screw lighters launched in the mid-1890s: *Vulcan* (1895) and *Hero* and *Victor* (1896). These three were the last iron screws to be built at the yard. The *Hero* figured in the news in the year after her launch when, on 4th February 1897, her boiler exploded at Bainsford, killing her skipper and engineer. She was brought back to Kirkintilloch where she was so well repaired by John Thom and his men that she continued to ply in the trade until 1948, when she was broken up at Kirkintilloch. Her sister ship *Victor* lasted until 1944, when she also was broken up at Kirkintilloch; but the *Vulcan* was sold to Fleetwood in 1920.[21] These boats seem to have been kept exclusively on Canal work until 1915 when, to meet a shortage of coasting boats, they were altered for coasting work and plied in the Firth of Clyde.[22]

In 1875, the year of the launching of the *Leopold*, the iron lighter *Ceres* was either converted to screw propulsion, if tradition is accepted, or built, if the entry in the Glasgow Port Registers is taken literally. With a gross tonnage of 38 and dimensions 65ft. × 13.7ft. × 4.6ft., she was in much the same class as the *Leopold* and, like her, could go into the Monkland Canal. Her single-cylinder engine of 12hp was installed at Port Dundas. She was sold to C. R. Dykes, Altrincham, in 1888.[23]

The yard had an interesting job in 1876 when it converted the *Agnes*, an old iron sloop built for the Canal Company in 1847 by Yule & Wilkie. James Hay bought her in 1865 and used her as a sailing barge on the Canal until 1876, when she was put into the yard at Kirkintilloch and prepared for a steam engine. The engine, a single-cylinder direct acting diagonal of 16hp, was installed by J. & J. Hay at Port Dundas. This was probably another experiment.

14

Arthur, an early 'shorehead' boat, built in 1877. She had tiller steering and was the only Hay boat to have a single-cylinder oscillating engine.

Photo courtesy J. M. Hay.

After conversion, the *Agnes* had a somewhat varied career and was finally wrecked off Cove on 13th October 1891. [24]

During the rest of the decade only two more screw lighters were built — the *Adelaide* (2), 58 gross tons, and the *Arthur*, 52 gross tons. *Arthur* appears to have been used for estuarial work; J. & J. Hay gave her a single-cylinder oscillating engine of 10hp — an experiment which served *Arthur* well enough until she foundered off Cove on 13th May, 1903, but which was not repeated, except in *La Belle*, an old puffer bought and re-engined by the Hays. *Adelaide* (2) had a 2-cylinder high-pressure direct acting engine of 10hp by Manderson, Hutson & Corbett — also something of an experiment. She was sold in 1881. [25]

During the decade of the 1870s the yard took on the general features which were to characterise it for the rest of its existence. The site lay on the south bank of the Canal, just west of the Townhead Bridge. There was a fairly flat plot of land, between 300 and 400 feet long and 60 feet broad, with a steep embankment rising on its southern boundary. The three sheds shown on the map of 1867 were replaced by a long shed containing most of the workshops and plant. Part of it was two-storied, with a moulding loft and a small office on the upper floor. Below, it was open on the Canal side and at its east end there was no upper storey. Here were stored templates and rivets. Under the moulding loft, on the Canal side, was the blacksmith's shop and opposite it, at the back of the shed, was the plate furnace. Beside the furnace were blocks and shaping frames and machinery for bending metal plates and belting for hulls. Extra belting at the bow was a common feature of the screw lighters built at the yard. There were also machines for cutting plates and punching holes in them, and a boring machine. In front of the blacksmith's shop, on open ground between it and the Canal bank lined by wooden wharfage, were the sawmill and sawpit. At the east end of the main shed were the carpenter's shop and tool shed and the paint store next to it. In 1903 a fire completely destroyed these sheds and damaged the main building. Thereafter the paint store was located at the west end of the yard, away from the sheds. At the east end of the yard was the building berth, with four large poles, one at each corner, to support the scaffolding. There was only one berth. Slipways were put down when the keel of a boat had been laid. The boat was jacked up on wedges. When she was ready for launching the

Hays' boatyard from the west. The nearer puffer is the *Zephon*, built in 1901 by Scott & Sons of Bowling for Munro & Findlay of Glasgow and acquired by J. Hay & Sons Ltd. in 1922.

wedges were knocked away from the centre outwards and she was allowed to settle on the slipway, which was heavily greased with tallow. At a word from the foreman, carpenters knocked out the pins that held the triggering mechanism and cut the last ropes holding the boat, and it went down into the Canal. From the beginning the boats were launched sideways and went in with a spectacular splash. Hawsers fore and aft arrested and held them when they were in the water. [26]

At the west end of the yard was a flat area where scows were drawn up on a slipway for overhauling and repairs. This was the slip referred to in the Canal Company's note of 1867 about water being taken from the Canal. After 1903 the paint store was located near this slipway, as was a latrine. There were no cranes in the yard. Manpower, with block and tackle, was able to do such lifting as was required. At Port Dundas a crane was available for fitting engines.

No detailed information about the work force at either Kirkintilloch or Port Dundas has been discovered. John Martin, writing in the early years of the 20th century, stated that between 20 and 30 men were employed at the Kirkintilloch yard. [27] The *Kirkintilloch Herald* of 1st November 1961 stated that in its peak years the yard employed thirty or more men. There seems to have been little change over the years in the numbers of the work force at the yard. It would be reasonable to conclude that as early as the 1870s twenty to thirty men were employed. Key men were the shipwrights, blacksmith and carpenter. Each would have some journeymen working with him and some apprentices; and there would be platers and riveters. Presumably the sawmill had a steam engine. This would require an engineer. There must always have been a nucleus of about ten journeymen and a dozen labourers to work with the craftsmen. John Thom, although officially styled 'Foreman Carpenter', was for all practical purposes Yard Manager; and that is how he is often described in press reports. John Thom's two sons, James and George, both worked at the yard. James was a patternmaker and joiner. George was a clerk doing general administrative work. The Thom family were closely associated with the yard for many years. Three generations of Thoms gave the firm long and valuable service. In this respect they emulated the Hay family. The whole concern was very much a Hay family business. Taking into account the initial venture of William Hay and his son, James, there was over a century of continuous control by members of the Hay family, with only one short break latterly. The launches at the yard were family gatherings of Kirkintilloch worthies, many of them related to the Hays, and all sharing the sense of having some connection with the yard. The work force had something of this family spirit, which made for good relations and good workmanship and encouraged pride in a yard which, by the end of the 1870s, had become an institution of the town. Launches, which could be viewed by members of the public from the Townhead Bridge and the Canal bank, were a popular feature of the life of Kirkintilloch at which the men of the yard provided spectacular entertainment.

At the end of the '70s occurred an event of considerable importance to the firm of J. & J. Hay. On the evening of 11th August 1879 James Hay set off to walk along the shore road from Dunoon to Kirn. He failed to arrive at Kirn. His body was found on the foreshore next morning. It was thought that he had fallen over the embankment, which at that point was eleven feet high.[28] John Hay, under the terms of the partnership, took over J. & J. Hay, including the boatbuilding yard. The firm retained its title. In practice there was little change, as far as the routine work of the yard was concerned. John Hay and John Thom continued to work together to keep the Hay fleet in serviceable order and to produce the types of vessel best suited to their needs. John Hay, however, now had control of finance and freighting in addition to his supervision of puffers and personnel, and in course of time found himself becoming involved in the fortunes of his brother's 'Strath Line', which had been taken over by James's son, Alexander Marshall Hay, who was less successful than his father. He had to leave more to John Thom in the working of the yard.

In the 1880s the British economy was taking an upward direction and there was plenty of scope for shipping. In spite of competition from the railways the Canal was busy. Timber and pig iron came in to Grangemouth and were sent

Two 'shorehead' puffers at the Townhead Bridge yard. The absence of bulwarks suggests that they were being used as 'inside' boats.

along the Canal to the west. Grain came down from north-east Scotland for the west coast distilleries. Coal was moved in both directions — to the West Highlands and Ireland, and also to the Continent. The Canal was involved in the initial stages in both directions. J. & J. Hay had a part in carrying all these various cargoes. The concern of the builders at the Kirkintilloch yard was to produce vessels which could deal with the cargoes most effectively.

As puffers evolved, three main types were emerging: the 'inside' boat, for canal work only; the 'shorehead' boat, which took in estuarial as well as canal work; and the outside boat, which was for coasting trade and went out into the open sea. The name of 'puffer' which covered them all originated with the early boats, which exhausted their engine through the funnel to help draughting. This caused a puffing noise and created the name. The inside boats, also known as canal screws or steam lighters, were a direct development from the horse-drawn lighter. They had no mast, no bulwarks, open hold, little freeboard, tiller steering. They were used first of all on the Canal only, and later for port lighterage; but they were not suitable for estuarial work or coasting. For such work a different type was required, with more freeboard; a mast, derrick and steam winch; hatch coamings and covers; bulwarks, wheel steering, which was of the chain and barrel type. Working conditions demanded sturdy hulls, which could stand up to constant running onto beaches to discharge cargoes. All the puffers, of whatever type, were single screw and had the engine and funnel at the stern. Shorehead boats derived their name from the 'Shorehead Limit' of the Clyde Estuary, from Skipness to Garrioch Head. Beyond this limit ships had to have 'loadlines', minimum freeboard, hatch-coamings, hatches and tarpaulins and locking bars. Boats operating inside the limit were not required to have these, although many of them had. They were known as 'shorehead' boats, although this term was officially frowned on. They were built to carry their maximum deadweight through the Canal and only sufficient cargo to be discharged in one day. They were smaller and shallower draughted than the coasting boats, and carried a crew of three, as against four in the coasters. They were robustly built for beach work and specifically designed for the Firth of Clyde. The coasting boats, in the initial stages of development, probably were influenced in their design by the gabbarts and schooners which had been carrying on the coasting trade. Some of the early coasters had two masts, for instance. But their later design was more in line with that of the shorehead boats, with modifications to suit their sea-going requirements. The early ships were flush-decked. Later ones had raised quarterdecks which, in the case of the outside boats, sometimes extended for a third of the vessel's length, giving greater buoyancy and more bunker room. Outside boats carried a trysail and sometimes a staysail also. [29]

It was in a background of these emergent types, with consideration for the various kinds of cargo involved, that John Hay and John Thom did their experiments in building at the Kirkintilloch yard. They were particularly concerned with the estuarial and coasting traffic and their designing was concentrated on these rather than on the inside Canal trade requirements.

Shorehead boats could be used as inside boats, but inside boats were limited to canal and port lighterage.

In the decade of the 1880s the yard had settled into its stride and had a very creditable output, turning out eleven vessels in all. *Lyra* and *Delta* were outside boats, 'the first positively identifiable', according to Mr. J. M. Hay, who described them as 'the recognisable progenitors of the long line of Hay coasting type puffers'.[30] *Leo, Albert* (2) and *Scotia* (2) were shorehead boats, *Beatrice* and *Alice* (2) were inside boats. Two iron lighters built in 1884 and one in 1886 were converted to steam, initially as inside boats. And at the end of the decade the yard built one of its most interesting ships — the *Aniline,* a tanker specifically designed for the carriage of tar in bulk. Building during the decade was largely experimental. Although it did not produce any types that were taken up, it gave the builders valuable experience on which to base further experiments.

The *Lyra* was launched on 4th September 1880, as reported in the *Lennox Herald* of 11th September 1880:

> On Saturday there was launched from the boatbuilding yard of Messrs. J & J Hay, Canal Bank, a beautiful steam lighter of over 100 tons. As the vessel slipped away from the blocks she was gracefully named the Lyra, of Kirkintilloch, by Miss Susan Stewart, Hillhead. Her machinery is to be supplied by Messrs. Hutson & Corbett, Kelvinhaugh, whence she will proceed forthwith, and when completed will be employed by the Messrs Hay in the large traffic carried on by them on the Forth and Clyde Canal. Just as the vessel left the blocks a sudden jerk caused one of the engineers from Glasgow, who was sitting on the edge of the bulwarks, to lose his hold, and he was thrown forward with considerable violence head-foremost into the hold, receiving a severe gash across the top of his head. Dr. Stewart advised his removal to the Infirmary.

Dr. Stewart was a well-established Kirkintilloch practitioner, said to be related to Archibald Stewart of the Waterloo Inn and connected by marriage with the Hay family. Susan Stewart was Archibald's daughter. The accident to the engineer was the only discordant note struck by the *Lyra* as she introduced a new phase and style into the fleet. James Hay's screw lighters — *Alice, Alfred, Arthur, Albert, Victoria, Adelaide* — had taken their names from members of the Royal family.[31] The style was continued under J. & J. Hay in *Louise* and *Leopold. Lyra* introduced a classical note with astronomical overtones. The next boat to be built was called *Leo.* Then came *Delta,* possibly named from Delta in the Belt of Orion, for she was followed by *Orion.* Just before *Delta* the firm had acquired the *Glasgow* of 1857 and had renamed her *Zeta,* another star in the Belt of Orion. *Argo* and *Neptune* completed this name series.

The *Delta,* 68 gross tones, was launched in December 1881. Between her launching and that of the *Lyra,* a smaller boat, the *Leo,* 51 gross tons, was built. Her launch was reported in the *Lennox Herald* of 25th June 1881. She was named by Miss Cameron, daughter of Provost Cameron, Southbank Iron

Works, who took a great interest in the yard and was a frequent guest at launches. His Iron Works was near the yard and there was probably a business connection.

Leo was given a single-cylinder high pressure direct acting engine of 18hp by J. & J. Hay at Port Dundas. She was used as a shorehead boat until she was wrecked in Saddell Bay on 16th January 1890.[32] She was replaced in 1892 by the *Argo,* of much the same dimensions, although of a greater tonnage; but no other shorehead boat of this type was built thereafter.

The year 1884 saw two large iron dumb lighters launched from the yard. Neither was registered; but one of them, the *Dinah,* was converted to steam in 1887 and was registered then in that name.[33] She ran on the Canal until 1891, when she was sold to Newcastle-on-Tyne. The other, whose name as a dumb lighter has not been traced, was sold in 1891 to James Glover of Paisley. She was fitted with a 2-cylinder compound engine of 12 NHP by Donald & Son of Johnstone, with a boiler by Wallace of Barrhead, and was registered in the name of *Craigielea.* As such, she became well known in the Firth of Clyde. She went to Newcastle upon Tyne in 1931, but returned to the Clyde some time later. She sank at her moorings at Greenock on 8th January 1950 and was written off as a constructive total loss.[34]

Another vessel which was built as a dumb lighter and then converted to a steam screw was the *Amy,* 43 gross tons, launched in 1886. In 1889 she was given a single-cylinder high pressure engine of 10hp by Fisher & Co. of Paisley. After some years as an inside boat she was registered in 1892 and used in the Firth of Clyde. In 1896 she sank in 60 feet of water off Fort Matilda, after a collision with MacBrayne's *Claymore.* One of her crew was drowned. The salvage squad from the yard raised her and brought her back to Kirkintilloch, where she was repaired. She returned to the Firth of Clyde, but foundered off Innellan in February 1899 and became a total loss.[35]

In 1886 also came the *Albert* (2), 53 gross tons. One of the earlier shorehead boats, she had a hull whose design derived from that of the inside boats, and was not unlike it; but she was fitted with cargo handling gear, hatch coamings and bulwarks. Her registry in the year of her launching shows that she was intended for shorehead work from the start. She had a single-cylinder high pressure direct acting engine of 16hp by Fisher & Co. of Paisley. This was replaced in 1914 by J. & J. Hay Ltd., who put in a 2-cylinder direct acting engine of 15hp. After an unspectacular but useful career she was dismantled for use as a coal hulk and her registry was closed on 10th January 1934.[36] She was still lying in Bowling Bay in 1951.

The *Scotia* (2) was launched in 1887. She was of similar dimensions to *Albert* (2), but of slightly greater tonnage and with a more powerful engine, single cylinder of 25hp, made and installed by J. & J. Hay at Port Dundas. She was a shorehead boat of the earlier type, and was used as such until she was broken up in 1921.[37] Two inside boats came out in 1888, the *Beatrice,* 39 gross tons, and the *Alice* (2), 44 gross tons. They were the last canal screws in the fleet to have the narrow hull required for entry into the Monkland Canal through the

Blackhill Locks. They were used in canal trade only. *Beatrice* went to London in 1904; *Alice* (2) was broken up in 1913.

The last launch from the yard in the decade was in September 1889 and was an unusual one in that the vessel launched had not been built for J. & J. Hay. She was built for Messrs James Ross & Co. of Limewharf Chemical Works, Falkirk, and was a pioneer in the field of carrying tar in bulk. This presented unusual problems of design and construction, and attracted some attention in shipbuilding circles. The designing seems to have been done by Gilbert Wilkie, whose Port Downie yard was near the Chemical Works. This yard had to be closed before the ship could be built there. Both Wilkie and Ross were on friendly terms with John Hay, and it was not difficult for them to arrange for the steamer to be built at Kirkintilloch by John Thom under Gilbert Wilkie's supervision. Wilkie had retired when his yard closed down and was in a position to work closely with John Thom. It is possible that his association with the yard started in this way.

The *Aniline* was launched on 28th September 1889. The *Kirkintilloch Herald* of 2nd October 1889 reported the launch at more length than usual:

> On Saturday afternoon Messrs J & J Hay launched from their yard, Southbank, Kirkintilloch, a steam lighter of a somewhat novel type. It has been built to the order of Messrs James Ross & Co, Lime Wharf Chemical Works, Falkirk, for conveying gas tar from the Glasgow Corporation Gas Works at Dawsholm to the Chemical Works at Falkirk. Hitherto the tar has been conveyed in casks, and it was to reduce the cost of transit that the expedient of constructing a vessel to convey it in bulk was resolved upon, and its execution entrusted to the Messrs Hay. Although previous experiments have been made in the way of fitting up tanks in vessels, this is the first time that a vessel has been wholly constructed for the purpose of carrying tar in bulk. The specialty is that the hull and two iron partitions at each end with a similar covering form a receptacle for the tar. To prevent the dangers likely to arise from the shifting character of the prospective cargo this large receptacle is divided into three tanks, which are connected by valves, so that the tar will flow in at one point by gravitation and be pumped out at one point on reaching the works at Falkirk. The vessel itself presented a very neat appearance, and was creditable to the builders and their Manager, Mr John Thom. It was built under the superintendance of Mr. Gilbert Wilkie, lately shipbuilder, Camelon. The launch was witnessed by a large number of invited guests and by a large number of uninvited spectators, who lined the banks of the canal and the bridge. The vessel as she left the ways was named 'Aniline' by Miss Sutherland, daughter of Mr. Robert Sutherland, Wallside, Falkirk.

The report continued with a list of those who attended the luncheon held after the launch in the moulding loft, catered for by R. F. Stuart of the Crown Restaurant. Among the guests was Samuel Crawford, taking time off from his duties as Yard Manager at J. & G. Thomson's Clydebank shipyard to revisit the yard whose inception owed so much to him. Another guest was Charles Stirling, a local manufacturer and an old friend of the Hay family, who recalled how 47 years previously he had been invited to the launch of a lighter for William Hay at Kelvin Dock. Ex-Provost Cameron was there. Also present was Thomas

Wilson, Canal Superintendant, and grandson of the Thomas Wilson who started it all when he built the *Vulcan*. J. & J. Hay were represented by William Moffat, William Hopkin and John Bow. William Moffat had worked in the office at Port Dundas from its inception, when his only assistant was an office boy. Members of the Fullarton family, who were building a ship for the Hay coasting fleet at Paisley, had come over with William Hay, eldest son of John Hay. And there were others, testifying to the widespread connections of J. & J. Hay. The yard was well established in the affections of the people of Kirkintilloch and was respected in its relations with other shipbuilding and engineering firms.

The activity of the yard during the decade emphasised its limitations. The slip at the west end of the yard could handle scows and lighters, and some of the smaller inside boats; but if several craft were requiring attention at the same time, some of them had to wait, or go elsewhere — to Gilbert Wilkie's slip dock

Delta on Hays' repair slip shortly after its opening in 1889. Built at Kirkintilloch in 1881, she was one of the earliest 'outside' boats in the fleet.

at Port Downie, or to the Swans' yard at Kelvin Dock, or to Robert Alexander's slip at Cuilhill, Baillieston, on the Monkland Canal. In 1888 Wilkie had to close the slip dock and yard at Port Downie because the site was required for railway expansion. Robert Alexander had already closed his slip at Cuilhill. These were blows to puffer owners using the Canal. J. & J. Hay were concerned: they had used these slips regularly. Their business was expanding. In 1888 John Hay had taken over his brother's coasting company from which he had begun to build a coasting company of his own, J. Hay & Sons. The time was ripe for an expansion of the Kirkintilloch yard. John Hay decided to approach the Caledonian Railway Company, who were proprietors of the Canal, for permission to build a slip dock on the south bank at the east side of the entrance to the Railway Basin, and to take in a plot of land adjacent to it for expansion of the yard by additional sheds and wharfage. In the summer of 1888 he wrote to James W. Clapperton, the Canal Agent for the Caledonian Railway Company, with the request that J. & J. Hay be allowed to build a slip dock with sheds and wharfage at this site.[38] In his letter he said:

> As this is a very important matter in the interests of the Canal on account of the demolition of Cuilhill and Port Downie slips, we hope you will give this your favourable consideration.

Clapperton replied, giving assent on behalf of the Railway Company and stating the terms of holding and the rent, which was £5 a year.[39] The terms permitted the building of a slip dock with a wharf on the Canal bank and sheds adjacent to the slip. The dock was about 70 feet long and 20 feet broad. The slip at the end of it was about the same length. Beyond it was a large shed which housed the engine and winch used for drawing vessels up onto the slip, which was fitted with a ratchet. The winch was originally worked by a steam engine, but after the Second World War an electrically-driven winch was substituted. The shed, which extended some distance back from the slipway, contained a foreman's office, a blacksmith's forge and shop, and machinery for punching, shearing and bending metal plates and bars. Alongside the slip was a shed where rivets and other metal parts were stored. The wharf beside the slip dock could be used for fitting out as well as for loading and unloading.

J. & J. Hay wasted no time in building this slip dock and extension to their yard. The *Kirkintilloch Herald* of 13th March 1889 reported completion of the work:

> On Saturday the first launch from the new slip of a 30-ton sloop took place, the 'Hercules' going smartly into the water end on.

The slipway was used for repair and overhaul work and, as far as is known, no ship was ever built there. The carriage could at a pinch accommodate two of the smaller or lighter ships, but the usual practice was to set up a vessel on blocks at the top end. The carriage was returned to the water and become available for a second vessel. It is believed that in cases where repairs were of a major or lengthy nature, the vessel could be side-stepped by means of hydraulic jacks, leaving the carriage free for other use. Latterly, of course, the proximity of

Southbank Road would have prevented this. The slipway was used also for breaking up the old and obsolete ships.[40]

In the 1890s the yard built its last inside boats and arrived at types of shorehead and outside boat which approximated to the firm's requirements and provided models on which later developments could be made to achieve the standard types. The first boat built in the decade was the *Orion*, 79 gross tons. She was an improved version of the *Lyra* and the *Delta*, built for the coasting trade. Her 2-cylinder compound tandem engine of 13hp, by Fisher & Co. of Paisley, was less powerful than those of the *Lyra* and the *Delta*. This may have contributed to her stranding near Arbroath on 11th November 1890. She was sold as a constructive total wreck. In the early part of 1891 she was given a temporary repair and was refloated; but when she was only five miles off Arbroath she foundered and was finally lost.[41] John Hay and John Thom must have been concerned about the design of this class of boat. No new building of screw lighters was done for at least a year, and they had time to think about it. The next one to be built was a shorehead type, the *Argo*, 61 gross tons. She was perhaps a replacement for the *Leo*, lost at the beginning of 1890; but her dimensions suggest that she was designed somewhat differently from the earlier shorehead boats. She was with the firm until 1906, when she was sold to James Warnock & Sons of Paisley, with whom she continued until the beginning of 1920 when she went to North Queensferry for breaking up.[42] Possibly Gilbert Wilkie had some influence in her design; but if so, it cannot have achieved the desired result. The first acceptable prototype of a Hay shorehead boat came two years later, in the *Celt*.

Launch of the *Nelson* at Hays' boatyard in 1893.

After the *Argo* the yard produced three coasting boats in succession, the *Neptune*, 80 gross tons, in 1892, and the *Nelson*, 81 gross tons, and the *Briton*, 83 gross tons, both in 1893. Their design was the basis of the standard Hay coasting puffers developed over the next three decades. They were fairly full forward, but had good curves in the run below water. They were not flat-bottomed, but had some rise, heavy bar-keels and round bilges. They had short raised quarter-decks. They were strongly built and could take a great deal of rough treatment. In November 1897 *Neptune* struck rocks on the south-east end of Arran and was beached on Pladda. Before she could be salvaged, bad weather drove her off and sank her. She was raised and taken back to Kirkintilloch by men of the yard. By May 1898 she was back in service. Unfortunately, she foundered off Islay less than four months after her return to work. In May 1898 *Nelson* went ashore on Black Head, Belfast Lough, and was thought to be a total wreck. She survived, however, as she did in the following year, when she had trouble with a cylinder off Sanda, when she was carrying a cargo of limestone. She reached Glenarm under sail, and was towed from there to Port Dundas for repair.[43] Gilbert Wilkie was undoubtedly involved in the designing of these boats. He and John Thom were toasted at the launching of the *Neptune*, reported in the *Kirkintilloch Herald* of 21st September 1892, as the men responsible for the *Neptune* and other vessels built at the yard.

The *Nelson* of 1893 was similar in engine and dimensions to the *Neptune* except that she had less depth of hold. She is thought to have been built for a specific trade. She was with the firm until 1924, when she was sold to Hughes, Blockow & Co. Ltd., North Shields. She was broken up in November 1956.[44]

The other vessel of 1893, the *Briton*, was the first of the series of coasting boats that carried the definitive stamp of the Kirkintilloch yard. She also initiated the 'tribal' pattern of naming which became a distinctive feature of Hay shorehead and outside puffers, and which was a particularly happy choice of name type, giving the boats a personality associated with the name which suited their style. The launch of this boat on 30th November 1893 was a more than ordinary occasion and was attended with more formality and ceremonial than usual. It was reported in the *Kirkintilloch Herald* of Wednesday, 6th December 1893:

On Thursday afternoon Messrs J & J Hay launched a screw steamer of 110 tons from their yard on the Forth and Clyde Canal at Kirkintilloch. The new vessel was a very smart looking craft and a credit to the builder, Mr. John Thom. . . . Among those present were — Rev. T. A. Morrison, Dr. Stewart and Captain Main, Kirkintilloch; ex-provost Rutherford, Lenzie; Mr John Hay of J & J Hay; Messrs Robert Harper, Cunningham, Robert Moffat, Barton, Robertson, George Milne, and Rankin Hay, Glasgow; Messrs Wm Moffat, Rankin and George Thom, of J & J Hay; Messrs Hunter and McNab, of J. Hay & Sons; Mr. Daly, of James Watson & Co.; Mr Riddell, Glasgow Gas Corporation; Mr. Donald, Flemington Coal Coy.; Capt. Mitchell, S.S. "Melmore"; Mr. David Kerr, of Colville, Loudon & Co; Mr. Buchanan of Ross & Duncan; Mr. Wallace, of John Wallace & Co., Barrhead; Messrs. Alex. Fullarton, James Fullarton and Alex Crawford, Paisley; Mr. Allan Marshall, Bridge of Allan; Messrs. James Hope (Nickel Works), Robert

Launch of *Briton* (1) at the Townhead Bridge yard on 30th November 1893.

Photo courtesy J. M. Hay.

Hudson (Lion Foundry), Charles Stirling (manufacturer), James Calder, James Stables, James Goodwin, John Cameron jun. and Inspector Gray, Kirkintilloch. When the company assembled, Miss Mary C. Cameron, Southbank House, the youngest daughter of ex-Provost Cameron, was conducted to the staging by Mr. Rankin Hay, and as the vessel glided off the ways the young lady christened her the "Briton", amidst the cheers of those in the yard and of the large crowd about the Bridge and the canal banks. . . . After the ceremony most of the invited guests ascended to the spacious yard loft where cake and wine were tastefully served by Mr. Wm. Muirhead. Mr. John Hay presided.

The list of guests shows the wide range of connections with John Hay. Rankin Hay, who led Miss Cameron to the staging, was John Hay's youngest son. He was aged sixteen and was an apprentice with the firm. In escorting Miss Cameron to the staging he was probably carrying out a custom general in Scottish yards at launches, whereby the youngest apprentice accompanies the lady who is performing the ceremony to the launching platform, where he presents her with a bouquet of flowers. Her duty in return is to take a flower from the bouquet and pin it in the apprentice's lapel. In the speeches after the

27

ceremony, James Fullarton said that in the *Briton* Mr. Hay thoroughly understood what he wanted and had a capable general in Mr. Thom. This is an interesting commentary on the relationship between John Hay and John Thom and their team work in producing exactly what they required. Later James Fullarton proposed the health of John Thom as 'the man who designed and built the ship'. He was quoted in the *Kirkintilloch Herald* as saying that 'there was no man, no matter what size of yard he was in, knew better what he was doing than Mr. Thom. The work here was small, but it was equally good to the biggest turned out on the Clyde or anywhere else'.

In spite of all the goodwill and optimism that surrounded the *Briton* at her launching, she did not last long with J. & J. Hay. She was sold to Newcastle upon Tyne on 26th January 1895. [45]

Another aspect of John Thom's work at the yard was well illustrated when the Company's puffer *Hannibal* sank in the Canal at Glasgow Bridge, west of Kirkintilloch, effectively blocking the passage for other vessels of any size. The *Kirkintilloch Herald* of 18th October 1893, reporting the incident, said:

> The boat had sunk in nine or ten feet of water, and with the exception of the funnel and stern rail was quite submerged in the centre of the waterway. Information of the accident was at once sent to Messrs. Hay and the Canal Company, and traffic in all but boats of a light draft was suspended. Early next morning preparations were made for having the vessel floated. A large number of iron plates had been prepared overnight at Messrs. Hays' yard at Kirkintilloch, and these were taken along and fixed round the gunwale of the submerged vessel, the deck area of which was then made watertight by a liberal use of puddled clay. The steam pump belonging to the Canal Company was then brought alongside, and commenced to pump out the water, and about three o'clock the vessel was floated and brought east to Kirkintilloch, after her cargo had been removed, where she will be put upon the slip for repair.

Sinkings in the Canal and elsewhere were not uncommon, and the yard had a special 'flying squad' to deal with them. Each case had to be dealt with according to its peculiar requirements. In November 1903, for instance, a scow sank at Hillhead. She was raised with some difficulty by the use of chains passed round her and attached to two other boats, one on each side, which were gradually lightened to bring her up. The episode was reported in the *Kirkintilloch Herald* of 18th November 1903. The repairing of the *Hero* after her boiler explosion in 1897 has already been mentioned; and there were many other accidents of one sort or another in which damaged vessels were put back in service by John Thom and his men. An interesting development of this activity of the yard was the buying of damaged or wrecked vessels of other owners at a low price, the repairing of them at Kirkintilloch, and either their sale at a profit or their entry into the Hay fleet. Sometimes the firm bought up vessels that were for sale in order to prevent them from being bought by someone else who might use them in competition with J. & J. Hay. The yard was used to put these vessels into the condition required for selling them to someone who would not be a competitor, or for trading under J. & J. Hay. This extension of the yard's work became a regular feature from the decade of the 1890s.

The year 1894 saw the introduction of the type of shorehead boat which, with minor variations, was to become standard in the fleet. The pioneer was the *Celt*, 58 gross tons, with a 2-cylinder engine of 25hp by J. & J. Hay. Her dimensions were somewhat different from those of the *Argo* and it is reasonable to assume that the design of the *Argo* had been abandoned in favour of that of the *Celt*. The *Celt* ran on the Canal and in the Firth of Clyde for twelve years. In 1906 she was sold to a Welsh company with headquarters at Port Madoc. She had been in collision with Wm. Robertson's *Kyanite* on 7th January 1905 in the stretch of the Firth between the Cloch and Toward Point — a wide area in which to have a collision. Her skipper was found to blame and the firm had to pay out some money. This may have been one reason for her sale. In 1920 she was taken over by the Admiralty and her registry was closed. [46]

After the *Celt* had cleared the stocks a consort to the *Briton* was laid down. The *Saxon* was launched on 4th October 1894. The *Glasgow Herald* of the following day reported that she had been named by 'a very young lady, Miss Kathie Stewart, of Westermains Cottage, Kirkintilloch'. The *Saxon* was identical with the *Briton* in dimensions and had a similar engine. She was registered at Glasgow in 1894, and ran in the coasting trade on the east coast. In the latter part of 1901 she was chartered to Murison & Campbell of Montrose and in the spring of 1902 she was sold to them. [47] In 1906 she went ashore in the Firth of Forth and was abandoned as a constructive total wreck. J. & J. Hay Ltd bought her cheaply from the underwriters, had her made seaworthy at Kirkintilloch, and brought her into their fleet once more. The Annual Report of the Directors for 1906 stated that:

> The Company's plant has been well maintained throughout the year, and remunerative repair work has been obtained at outside vessels and carried out at Kirkintilloch.

This appears to refer to the *Saxon*, and does not indicate a policy of opening the yard to repairs for outside firms. A problem of nomenclature was raised with the *Saxon*'s return to the fleet. In 1904 a second *Saxon* had been built. She was renamed *Gascon* when *Saxon* (1) came back. *Saxon* (1) was in collision with the Norwegian steamer *Waterloo* off Pladda on 24th October 1912 and sank with the loss of two lives. [48]

The last of the flush-decked inside boats to be built at the yard were the *Vulcan* (1895) and the *Hero* and *Victor* (1896). *Victor* was the last iron screw lighter to come from the yard, which had gone over to building in steel. The only subsequent buildings in iron were two horse scows, launched in 1902. [49] *Vulcan*, *Hero* and *Victor* all underwent conversion in 1915 when they were altered for coasting work, to meet a shortage of coasting boats brought about by Admiralty requisitions. They seem to have been satisfactory in their new role, and were not reconverted after the war. [50]

In addition to the *Vulcan*, the yard in 1895 built the *Norman*, an outside coasting boat in all respects identical to the *Saxon* of the previous year. She was a good boat, giving long service. On 11th December 1912 she was driven ashore at Turnberry in a gale and lay on the rocks for almost a month. She was brought

Launch of the *Victor*, the last iron screw lighter to come from Hays' yard, on 4th November 1896.

off by the Glasgow Salvage Association and was repaired at Kirkintilloch. In 1914 she was chartered to the Admiralty, along with the *Briton* (4), for service at Cromarty, and remained there until after the Armistice. In 1930 she was sold to the Arran Shipping Company, went to Rothesay owners in 1935 and was broken up in 1953.[51] The *Norman* was followed by the *Briton* (2) in 1896 — a busy year for the yard, which built the *Hero* and the *Victor* as well — and by the *Gael* in 1897. The pattern for the outside boats was set for the time being. *Briton* (2) was the first steel vessel built in the yard. She was launched on 31st July 1896. The *Kirkintilloch Herald* of 5th August 1896, reporting her launch, commented on the prosperity of the yard:

> There is no more active industry in Kirkintilloch than boat building, the continuity of launches in Messrs Hay's yard keeping the men engaged there in constant employment. The latest launch was on Friday, when the Briton was consigned to her native element . . . as she slid down the ways she was christened the "Briton" by Miss Roberta Watson Anderson, daughter of Mr. G. L. Anderson, Oxford Cottage, Kirkintilloch.

Gael (1) of 1897.

G. L. Anderson was a well-known local chemist and a neighbour of John Thom. The town was proud of the little yard on the Canal, which was turning out ships designed and built by Kirkintilloch men, more often than not manned by Kirkintilloch crews, and carrying the good repute of Kirkintilloch shipbuilding up and down the coasts of Scotland. Unfortunately, *Briton* (2) did very little of this. She foundered off Copeland less than a year after her launch. The *Gael* which followed her in 1897 and was the last of the class had a life span of thirty years. She was wrecked on the Small Isles, Jura, on 28th January 1927 and became a total loss. [52] Her lifetime was not without incident. In her first year she grounded on the Annat Bank at Montrose, but was refloated. Two years later she lost her propellor off Wemyss Bay but managed to reach Bowling under sail, where she was beached and had a new propellor and shaft fitted. On 11th February 1906 she was driven ashore at Port Ellen, Islay, and almost became a total loss. She was salved and brought back to Bowling, where she was slipped. There she was written off as a total loss and the underwriters paid for her as such. Messrs. J. & J. Hay Ltd. bought her from the underwriters for £540, took her to the yard at Kirkintilloch and rebuilt her. Three years later she was in collision in the Firth of Forth with the *Staffa* of the Currie Line and was badly damaged. Again she was brought back to Kirkintilloch, was slipped and repaired, and resumed service.[53] John Thom had built a good ship in her.

J. & J. Hay Ltd. (1896-1921)

The prosperity reflected in the activity at the boatyard was the background to a development in J. & J. Hay. John Hay had been for almost twenty years the sole survivor of the partnership. In 1890 he had set up a separate company, J. Hay & Sons, to continue the coasting business of his brother James. He felt that it was time that a clear division was made between the two concerns and that J. & J. Hay was put on a formal basis as a limited company. In 1896 John Hay arranged to sell the business and property of J. & J. Hay to a new company, J. & J. Hay Ltd., having a share capital of £50,000, divided into 2000 five per cent cumulative preference shares of £10 each and 3000 ordinary shares of £10 each. The business was sold on 1st September 1896. The directors of the new company were as follows:

John Hay, Managing Director, 58 Renfield Street, Glasgow, and Port Dundas.
John Neilson (Neilson Brothers), Iron and Steel Merchant, Glasgow.
Richard G. Ross (R. G. Ross & Son), Engineer, Glasgow.
William Beardmore (William Beardmore & Company, Parkhead Forge, Glasgow).
William Hay, 58 Renfield Street, Glasgow.

John Hay Jr. was the Secretary. He and William were sons of John Hay.

The property sold included 'the Fittings and Fixtures of the Boatbuilding Yard, Repairing Slips, Forge, Engineers' and Boilermakers' Shops . . .'[54] Referring to the Hay fleet, the Prospectus stated:

All the Coasting Steamers, Steam Lighters and Barges are of iron or steel, and are built especially for trading on the Canal, and certain of the steamers are employed on the estuaries of the Clyde and the Forth, while others trade between the Canal and West Highlands of Scotland, Belfast, Larne, etc., on the west, and Aberdeen, Montrose, Arbroath, Dundee, Newcastle, etc., on the east coast.

The ground is leased from the Caledonian Railway Company, who own the Canal. The Vendor has expended considerable sums on the erection of buildings thereon, etc., and the Boatbuilding Yard and its accessories enable repairing to be executed promptly and at first cost, which is a matter of considerable moment. The Vendor claims the fixtures, which are valued by Mr. John Anderson, valuator, at £2760, and the Vendor's rights therein are acquired by the Company.

The Shipping property has been valued by Mr. Gilbert Wilkie, boatbuilder, Falkirk, at £20,536 5s 0d. . . .[55]

John Hay had brought in as Directors three old friends whose technical knowledge as well as business acumen was likely to benefit the new company; and he could rely on good relations with them. It is interesting to note Gilbert Wilkie's involvement in valuing the shipping, indicating that he was still keeping contact with the firm. The Repairing Slips referred to were the one at the slip dock of 1889 and the older one at the west end of the Townhead Bridge Yard. *Briton* (2) would be on the stocks when the prospectus was being drafted. As she was the first steel vessel to come from the yard, it is clear that the decision to build in steel had been taken before the formation of the new company, and so was not a result of its formation.

The new company built no more inside boats. The emphasis was on the coasting trade. Two new classes of coasting boat were developed, one in the 89-92 gross tons range, the other in the 68-69 gross tons range. A slightly smaller shorehead class was also brought out, with boats in the 64-65 tons range. The smaller coasting class could combine estuarial with coasting work, while the shorehead boats could be used on the Canal as inside boats, with their midship bulwarks removed.

After the launch of the *Gael* in the summer of 1897 the first of the improved outside boats was laid down. She was called *Tartar* and gave her name to the new class. Later boats in it were described as 'Tartar type'.[56] *Tartar* was a steel screw steamer of 89 gross tons, with a 2-cylinder compound engine of 17hp by Ross & Duncan of Govan, the boiler being by J. Wallace & Co., Barrhead. She was launched at the end of 1897. In her first year of service she brought her owners some salvage money when she took in tow the three-masted schooner, *Silvia,* in difficulties off Islay. Otherwise, she had an uneventful life, giving half a century of work for the Company until she was broken up in 1947. She was followed by the coasting boats *Druid,* 92 gross tons, in 1899, and *Moor,* 89 gross tons, in 1901. *Druid* foundered off Island Magee on 14th June 1905. *Moor* foundered at the mouth of the Tay on 23rd December 1915.[57] It has been suggested that the *Moor* was built to the design and specifications of Scott & Co. of Bowling. In December 1898 John Hay had an informal conversation with the Company which resulted in a verbal offer from them to build 'another hull similar to the one the directors agreed at the last meeting to commence at Kirkintilloch'. The vessel was to be ready in June 1899.[58] The boat agreed by the Directors had been the coasting vessel *Druid.* It is assumed that the boat agreed with Scott & Co. was similar. In May 1899 it was reported that Scott & Co. had not even started the boat. It was arranged that the contract be cancelled, the material be taken over by J. & J. Hay Ltd. and the boat built at Kirkintilloch.[59] The next coasting boat to come from the yard was the *Moor.* Her dimensions, however, did not tally with those shown in Scott & Co.'s specification, and it is not clear whether she was built according to it or to the specifications for the *Tartar* class of boats, as her dimensions, tonnage and engine suggest. Possibly J. & J. Hay were more interested in obtaining a design from Scott & Co. than in having them build a boat. In later years, they frequently went to Scott & Co. for drawings to their specifications and

Tartar at Custom House Quay, Glasgow. Built in 1897, she initiated a new class of 'outside' boat.

G. E. Langmuir.

established a useful contact with the Bowling firm. The design of the *Tartar* class boats, however, does not seem to have been affected.

The year 1898 saw the first of the smaller class of coasting boat, the *Dane,* 69 gross tons, with a 2-cylinder engine of 25hp supplied by J. & J. Hay Ltd. She was reported as being a popular type of boat and gave her name to the smaller coasting class, as the *Tartar* had to the larger one. [60] She was sold to R. Inglis of Leith in 1902, went on to the Perth Shipping Company in 1905 and returned to the Clyde when James Warnock bought her in 1906. Some years later she featured in a gruesome incident. The *Glasgow Herald* of 6th April 1914 reported that on the previous day her crew came aboard early in the morning as she lay in Paisley harbour, her furnace damped down. When they stoked it to raise steam smoke poured out through the furnace door. Probing the funnel for an obstruction, they found the remains of a human body. How it came there was never discovered, and the identity of the individual was never found out. The *Dane* was sold to Richard Irvin & Sons of North Shields in 1929.[61] The next shorehead boat to be built was the *Turk*, 65 gross tons, launched in 1900. She was sold to Limerick in 1911.[62]

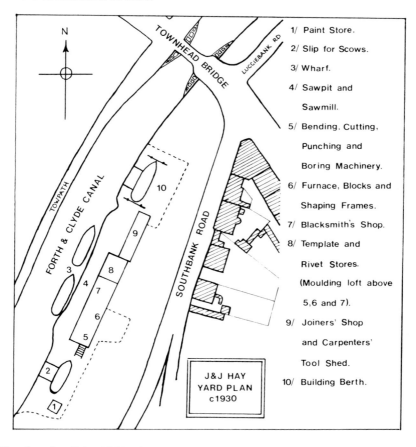

1/ Paint Store.

2/ Slip for Scows.

3/ Wharf.

4/ Sawpit and Sawmill.

5/ Bending. Cutting, Punching and Boring Machinery.

6/ Furnace, Blocks and Shaping Frames.

7/ Blacksmith's Shop.

8/ Template and Rivet Stores. (Moulding loft above 5,6 and 7).

9/ Joiners' Shop and Carpenters' Tool Shed.

10/ Building Berth.

J&J HAY YARD PLAN c1930

The decade of the 1890s, in addition to initiating important new types of ship and bringing in the new administration that grew up with the start of J. & J. Hay Ltd., saw an event of great concern for the Kirkintilloch yard. On 9th April

1898 John Thom died, at the age of fifty-six. From the yard's earliest days his influence had been the dominant one in its day-to-day running. Indeed, he was sometimes referred to as the Father of Shipbuilding at Kirkintilloch. His influence had been felt also in the wider matters of planning and design. He was officially described as 'Foreman Carpenter', but in effect he was Yard Manager. His part in the planning and designing was probably linked closely with that of Gilbert Wilkie; there is no record of the yard having a designer on its staff. But it was John Thom who built the ships. He was a good practical workman, who had very little recourse to the drawing board, working largely by rule of thumb. No drawings or even lines of any vessel built by John Thom have been found; but he knew exactly what he wanted and how to produce it, and the end product carried a high standard of workmanship. In the broad context his achievement was considerable. He thought big and built solidly, with strong, sound materials that produced vessels to last. It used to be said in the Glasgow office that at the Kirkintilloch yard everything had to be on a large scale; nothing less than a six-inch nail would do, and nuts and bolts had to have at least ten washers. John Thom's personal supervision ensured that the best quality of materials and workmanship went into the vessels he built. The long life of those which survived natural calamities or accidents was testimony to the high standard of workmanship which he obtained from his work force. Critical in his assessment of work and sparing in his commendations, it is said that a sign of his highest approval was the remark 'Aye, we'll mak it dae.'' He designed and built to the requirements of the firm. The types of ship which he had been developing and was introducing at the time of his death were outstanding in their lines and performance. John Thom, like many practical engineers, had a streak of the artist in him. His boats had good lines and a well-balanced, harmonious structure, which appeared to best effect, perhaps, at launches, when their harmony was enhanced by their freshness.

John Thom's death raised the question of a successor. The problem was solved by a dual appointment. There was little delay: the *Kirkintilloch Herald* of 11th May 1898 reported:

> Mr. Geo. Thom has, we understand, been appointed Manager and Mr. John Gray, Foreman, at Messrs. J. & J. Hays' boatbuilding yard, in room of the late Mr. John Thom.

John Gray had been Foreman at Port Dundas. His qualifications to take John Thom's place in the yard are not clear; he left Kirkintilloch about 1911 or 1912 to go to America, and on his return, before the First World War, he went to Peter McGregor's yard as a shipwright, which suggests that he had some experience in practical shipbuilding. It was perhaps uncertainty about John Gray's ability to follow John Thom's planning and designing that led John Hay to make his informal approach to Scott & Co. of Bowling. The new arrangement, however, came into force with no apparent disruption and continued successfully for some time. George Thom's younger brother James continued to work as patternmaker and joiner. Not long after his father's death he was involved in a Canal rescue. The *Kirkintilloch Herald* of 24th August 1898 described it:

On Thursday evening, while Mr James Thom, joiner, was at work in the west slip of Messrs J. & J. Hays' boat-building yard his attention was directed to a boy who had fallen into the canal and was in great danger of being drowned. Without divesting himself of his clothing, Mr Thom jumped into the water and swimming across the canal managed to grasp the boy by the hand as he was sinking, and brought him to the bank. The little fellow, who is the son of Mr Alex Knox, secretary of the Rechabite Band, was conveyed home to his parents' residence in Brierybank Buildings, Townhead Street, and we are glad to learn is none the worse of his immersion.

We are not told how James Thom fared after *his* immersion. Being a Thom, he probably went back and finished his work before going home to change his clothes.

The *Dane* was John Thom's last ship. George started his regime with *Druid* of 1899, a coasting boat of 92 gross tons, the largest so far built at the yard. She had a short career with the Company; she foundered inexplicably off Island Magee, in Larne Lough, on 15th June 1905. [63]

In the summer of 1899 the yard began a series of repair jobs on vessels bought from other owners which brought some profit and some additions to the fleet. The first was the *Lookout,* an old puffer built in 1868 at Blackhill, which was bought for £115, was overhauled in the yard and sold to William Taylor of Grangemouth for £200. [64] In the next three years the Company bought cheaply three coasting boats, similar to the *Tartar* class, which had all been wrecked and badly damaged — *Roslin Glen, Macnab* and *Dorothy*. They were all repaired at Kirkintilloch and put into service with J. & J. Hay Ltd. The first of the three, the *Roslin Glen,* was renamed *Briton*. A Minute of the meeting of Directors held on 27th October 1899 stated that:

The Directors also agreed to alter the name of the "Roslin Glen" to "Briton" to conform with the names of the other vessels.

This is the first indication of a definite policy in naming the boats in the "tribal" pattern. The *Macnab* was similarly repaired in 1901 and was brought into service as the *Spartan*. The *Dorothy,* which had been wrecked in 1902, retained her name when she came off the slip at Kirkintilloch. *Briton* (3), *ex-Roslin Glen,* was sold in 1905, but continued working for various owners on the east coast until she was broken up at Grimsby in 1928. *Spartan, ex-Macnab,* remained with the Hays until 1923, when she was sold to a French owner and renamed *City of Calais*. The *Dorothy* was at Scapa during World War I. She returned to John Hay & Sons Ltd and worked for them until she was lost by stranding at Castlebay, Barra, in 1938. [65]

The year 1900 saw two sinkings in the Canal, the *Hannibal* and the *Celt*. The salvage squad from the yard raised them both by the pumping process previously used when the *Hannibal* sank in 1893. [66]. In 1900 also a new gas engine for driving machinery in the shop at Port Dundas was installed, and the Directors arranged to have it drive a dynamo which supplied electric light in the Company's premises there. There is no indication that a similar arrangement was made at the Kirkintilloch yard. After the *Turk* of 1900 and the *Moor* of 1901 came the *Greek*, a shorehead type of boat of 64 gross tons. She was launched on 12th June 1902, being named by Miss Maggie F. Cochrane, daughter of Parish Councillor Cochrane of Ashgrove Cottage. The *Kirkintilloch Herald* of 18th June 1902 recorded the event. *Greek* was the first shorehead boat to have her boiler from J. Wallace & Co., who thereafter supplied all boilers up to the end of the 1920s.

On 30th August 1902 the yard launched an iron scow. The *Kirkintilloch Herald* of 3rd September 1902 commented that this was the first boat of its kind built at the yard for 30 years. The figure of 30 years is open to question, but there is no doubt that scow building at the yard had been in abeyance for some time. The Company's policy seems to have been to buy scows and barges from other owners. In 1897, for instance, they bought two scows from James Wood Ltd. In the previous year they had had two barges built by D. M. Cumming at

Saxon (3) at Millport on 29th August 1965. Built as *Dane* (2) in 1903 and renamed *Saxon* in 1914, she was operated by Kerr of Millport between 1925 and 1967.

Don Martin.

Blackhill. The building of the scow at Kirkintilloch was unusual. It was followed by the building of a second scow; but thereafter was not repeated. [67]

In the early part of 1903 a fire, starting in the paint shed, blazed up quickly and spread to the carpenter's shop and tool shed and then to the main building. By the time that it was under control the paint shed and carpenters' shop and shed had been completely destroyed and the main shed partly burned. Damage was estimated at over £300. When the buildings were replaced, the paint shed was moved to the west end of the yard away from the other buildings. The setback was temporary; the next vessel to be completed was launched on 28th August 1903. She was the *Dane* (2), 64 gross tons. The launch was reported in the *Kirkintilloch Herald* of 2nd September 1903, which described her as a sister ship to the *Greek*. In her early years she ran on the Canal as an inside boat, unregistered. In 1914 she was registered in the name of *Saxon*. *Saxon* (1) had been sunk two years before; *Saxon* (2) had been renamed *Gascon* in 1907; *Dane* (1) was back in the Clyde, in Warnock's fleet. It was perhaps to avoid confusion with her that *Dane* (2) was renamed *Saxon*. She suffered the same fate as *Saxon* (1) when she was sunk off Greenock on 3rd December 1925. She was sold where she lay to Finlay and Walter Kerr of Millport, who raised her, repaired her and re-registered her on 25th May 1926 as *Saxon*. She served them for another 40 years, in the course of which she became the first puffer to star in a television series, as the *Vital Spark* (unregistered). In this role she brought the name and personality of puffers to thousands who might otherwise have known nothing about them. She was broken up in 1967. [68]

Two boats, one coasting, one shorehead, were built in 1904: the *Roman*, 69 gross tons, launched on 22nd January 1904; and the *Saxon* (2), 64 gross tons, launched on 8th July 1904. Both were fitted with hatch coamings and covers, although initially they were used on the Canal only, and had the midship section of their bulwarks omitted. This was the case with the *Greek* and the *Dane* (2) also. When they were registered — *Saxon* (2) as *Gascon* in 1911, the others in 1914, with *Dane* (2) as *Saxon* (3) — all were fitted with bulwarks for estuarial work. *Gascon* was sold in 1913 to the Millom & Askam Hematite Iron Company. [69] The *Greek*, in her latter days, was used to carry bunker coal to Clyde Trust dredgers and hoppers, and reverted to the status of an inside boat, with wheel steering replaced by a tiller and bulwarks once more removed. She was broken up in 1953. The *Roman* was a familiar sight in the Firth of Clyde. She was sold to the Arran Shipping Co. in 1935 and her registry was transferred to Irvine. She was broken up in 1958.

The year 1905 opened with repair work at the slip on the *Greek*, which had been in collision with the Greenock Towing Co.'s tug *Commodore* on 3rd December 1904, followed by repair work on the *Celt*, after a collision with the *Kyanite* of Wm. Robertson on 7th January 1905. [70] Nonetheless, the yard was able to launch three boats during the year. *Briton* (4), 68 gross tons, was launched on 4th March 1905; *Trojan*, 65 gross tons, on 27th July 1905; and *Druid* (2), 68 gross tons, on 2nd December 1905. She replaced *Druid* (1), lost in the previous June. The *Kirkintilloch Herald* of 6th December 1905, reporting her launch, commented:

> The last year has been a busy one at the yard, the tonnage put out having exceeded any former year. Two large boats and a small one have been put into the water, the previous best having been one large boat and two small ones. In addition to this the yard has to undertake the repair work upon the large fleet owned by Messrs Hay.

Of these three boats, *Briton* (4) was with the Company for a quarter of a century. During the First World War she was chartered to the Admiralty at Cromarty. She was sunk in a collision seven miles off Campbeltown on 18th February 1931.[71] The *Trojan* had a long record of solid, useful service which continued until she was broken up in 1953.[72] *Druid* (2), like *Briton* (4), was used in the coasting trade. In 1912 she went ashore at Fair Head, for a few hours. She put into Ballycastle to discharge her cargo and a repair squad was sent out from Kirkintilloch to make temporary repairs. She had considerable damage, but was made seaworthy at the yard and was soon in service again. In 1915 she was requisitioned by the Admiralty for service at Scapa Flow, and was there until 1919. She continued on coasting work right through the Second World War. In 1953 she was equipped with a radio telephone, an improvement introduced in the 1950's to several of the coasting boats by Mr J. M. Hay, Chairman and Managing Director of the Company. She was sold on 10th August 1955 to R. J. Soutar of Stirling, who renamed her *Kippen*. She was broken up at Troon in 1959.[73]

During 1906 there was so much repair work at the yard that no building was done. The *Gael,* which had been written off as a total loss and had been bought as a wreck, was rebuilt at the yard; and much the same thing was done with the *Saxon* (1). On 28th December 1906 the *Spartan* went ashore at Bowmore, Islay, and had to be towed back to Kirkintilloch, where she was given extensive repairs.[74] On 20th March 1907 the yard launched the *Celt* (2), 69 gross tons. She was a steady, reliable vessel which worked for the Company for the better part of half a century, except for a period of war service between 1914 and 1919, when she was at Rosyth, under requisition by the Admiralty. She was dismantled in 1953 and used as a hulk.[75]

With the launching of *Celt* (2) J. & J. Hay Ltd. completed their series of smaller coasting boats. No other boat in this class was built until after the First World War. In the period between 1907 and 1914 two more coasting boats came from the yard — the *Cossack*, 92 gross tons, in 1908 and the *Cretan*, also 92 gross tons, in 1910. Both were chartered to the Admiralty in August 1914, for service at Cromarty, and remained there until 1919. *Cossack* was sunk off Islay on 13th June 1923. *Cretan* was wrecked in Loch na Keal, Mull, on 6th January 1939 and was written off as a constructive total loss.[76] After the launch of the *Cretan* only one ship was built until well after the end of the First World War. This was the *Serb*, 93 gross tons, an outside coaster which came from the yard in 1916. At the end of the year she was chartered to Wm. Baird & Co. for trading in the West Highlands, by arrangement with the Ministry of Munitions. After the war she returned to the Company's service, but was lost by stranding off Ardbeg, Islay, on 4th December 1925.[77]

In the years immediately leading up to the outbreak of the First World War trade on the Canal and on the Firths was booming and the yard at Kirkintilloch was kept fully occupied overhauling and repairing the numerous vessels in the Company's puffer and lighter fleets. In 1910 the Directors decided not to build any new vessels for the time being, "but to spend some time overhauling barges and coasting boats presently trading".[78] The *Kirkintilloch Herald Annual* for 1913 stated:

> Messrs. J. & J. Hays' men have been kept so busy at repair work that they have been unable to find time for the laying of the keel of a new boat, which has been decided upon.

It was going to be several years before that boat was built.

In 1910 George Thom had become Shipping Manager for J. & J. Hay Ltd., with his office in Glasgow. He continued to live in Kirkintilloch, where he moved into 'Dalblair', off Northbank Road, and kept a supervisory eye on the administration of the yard. When John Gray went to America, his place as Foreman was taken by Robert Miller, a carpenter at the yard. Robert Miller held the post right through the war, relinquishing it in the early 1920s, when James Thom took his place.

By 1912 the design of the coasting boats seems to have been settled and it was agreed at a meeting of the Directors in January of that year that a set of drawings of each of the two latest types of coasting lighter should be prepared. At the next meeting, however, it was decided:

> to defer having the sets of drawings made out as arranged at last meeting owing to the sudden development of motor boat orders and possible necessary alteration of design.[79]

In 1912 experiments with 'motor puffers' were being made, and several were built at the yard of Peter McGregor & Sons at Kirkintilloch. J. & J. Hay Ltd. were obviously watching this new development. They decided not to become involved; their decision was minuted at a meeting held on 26th November 1912:

> It was considered premature to adopt motor propulsion yet.

Subsequent developments justified their decision: the motor coasters were not a success. The outbreak of war in 1914 had a dramatic effect on trade. This is reflected in the Company's Minutes:

> Traffic was reported as having suddenly dropped very seriously owing to the European War. The coasting lighters had with difficulty been kept moving but traffic in that direction also had a disappearing tendency and it was feared partial laying-up at least might have to be resorted to (31st August 1914).
> Owing to the closing of the River Forth for general navigation it was anticipated that inland traffic would completely cease when the timber steamers presently working had been cleared (27th November 1914).
> Traffic was reported as having come to a standstill as far as inland work was concerned (28th December 1914).

Cretan, Cossack, Norman and *Briton* (4) all went off on charters to the Admiralty. *Druid* (2) and *Dorothy* went in the following year, and the old inside boats *Vulcan, Hero* and *Victor* were altered for coasting work, as was the

Hannibal. Moor was carrying a boiler for the Admiralty when she foundered at the end of 1915.

In 1915 the Company lost John Hay, the last surviving member of the original business of William and James Hay. He died on 18th August 1915. His influence was stamped on every aspect of the Company's affairs. The Company owed its character largely to him; and in no branch more so than in the 'puffers', whose individualism reflected his imagination and enterprise. Right to the end of his days he took a particular interest in these vessels and in the men who built and manned them. Even the distinctive pink of their funnels owed its concept to him. The story in the Company was that red lead was originally used on the funnels. Another company was doing this also, and objected to the Hays doing so. John Hay found that there was a large supply of white paint in the yard at Kirkintilloch. He had this mixed with the red lead, to produce the colour that was distinctive to all subsequent Hay puffers. In his last few years, John Hay delegated much of his work to his elder son, William. William succeeded him as Chairman of J. & J. Hay Ltd. and J. Hay & Sons. John, the younger son, who had been made a Director in 1902 after the resignation of John Neilson some time before, became Managing Director of J. & J. Hay Ltd., in which capacity he showed much of the character and ability of his father.

By 1916 trade was almost at a standstill. Most of the horse scows and barges were laid up. In the summer three were taken for Government work at the Forth Bridge and Rosyth.[80] The Company were glad to charter the *Serb* at the end of the year.

In 1917 the Admiralty were considering a scheme for the transport of oil on a considerable scale between Bowling and Grangemouth. The scheme was to be managed by the Inland Water Transport Service, and J. & J. Hay Ltd. were to play a big part in it. Horse barges and some screw lighters were to be converted by fitting tanks for the oil. This work was put in hand at the yard, where 12 barges were converted, as was the steam lighter *Terrier*. By the next year the Admiralty had decided to lay a pipe line instead; so the converted vessels had only a limited use. In 1918, however, the Admiralty took over more scows and the steam lighter *Caesar,* for work on the Canal in connection with the pipe line and for other purposes.[81] There was very little for the yard to do until the vessels were returned after the cessation of hostilities.

J. Hay & Sons Ltd. (1921-1956)

By the time that the steamers and lighters on war service had been returned and overhauled for normal working, the first signs of a decline in trade on the Canal were becoming apparent. The shipyards on it were either closing down or were functioning on a very limited scale. The only fully operational yard on the Forth and Clyde Canal was that of J. & J. Hay Ltd. at Kirkintilloch. This was largely due to the fact that it did not rely on outside orders to keep it going. Road and rail transport were successfully challenging canal transport, which was being

43

John Hay (1837-1915).

Photo courtesy J. M. Hay.

Launch of the Serb (2) on 23rd September 1927.

steadily cut down. The Hays' vessels, operating from Kirkintilloch as their home port, became the main users of the Canal. The yard based its continuance on their requirements. None the less, the Directors of J. & J. Hay Ltd. felt that in the interests of economy and efficient administration the Company should be absorbed into J. Hay & Sons as a subsidiary. Negotiations for this started in 1920 and were completed in 1921. The new amalgamated group was known as J. Hay & Sons Ltd. The yard at Kirkintilloch, along with the puffer fleet, the horse-drawn scows and the engineering works at Port Dundas, all came under its control. William Hay, who was Chairman and Managing Director, retired in 1923 and was succeeded in these offices by his brother John who continued to hold them until his death in 1948. George Thom became General Manager of the new company, with headquarters at 58 Renfield Street, Glasgow. His brother James took over the yard at Kirkintilloch from Robert Miller. This facilitated George Thom's contact with the yard. It is related that in the early morning he used to come down to the Canal from his house on the North Bank. James met him with a punt and took him across to the yard. He and George went round it together, and then George went off to Glasgow. [82] The yard was fortunate in obtaining the services of Jock Wardlaw, a very skilled blacksmith, who had worked for Peter McGregor & Sons and had been made redundant when they went out of business in 1921.

Building at the yard did not re-start until 1924, when it was decided to make up for the sale of the *Nelson* that year and the loss of the *Cossack* in 1922 by a large coasting boat. She was the *Moor* (2), 97 gross tons, the largest vessel built so far at the yard. She was launched in January 1925 and worked until 1956, when she was dismantled and used as a hulk. [83]

The *Serb* of 1916 stranded off Ardbeg, Islay, on 4th December 1925 and became a total wreck. The *Gael* of 1897, one of the older type of coasting boats, was wrecked on the Small Isles, Jura, on 18th January 1927. These two were replaced by the *Serb* (2), 95 gross tons, which was launched on 23rd September 1927. The *Kirkintilloch Herald* of Wednesday, 28th September 1927, reported the launch:

> From their boat-building yard at Kirkintilloch on Friday afternoon Messrs J. Hay & Sons Ltd. launched the steam lighter "Serb", which is to be employed in their own coastal traffic. The launch was timed for 3 o'clock and there was not the usual crowd of school children about. There was a big gallery of adults, however, at the Canal bridge and in Southbank Road. The operations were superintended by Mr James Thom, the yard foreman, with Mr. George Thom representing the owners, and were carried out without a hitch, the boat taking the water in the sweetest possible manner.

Serb (2) was the last vessel from the yard to have her boiler from J. Wallace & Co. She was with J. Hay & Sons Ltd. until 1958, when she was sold to A. M. Lamond of Perth and renamed *Foam*. [84]

Both *Moor* (2) and *Serb* (2) were improved versions of the *Tartar* class. Only one more vessel of this type was built — the *Tuscan*, 93 gross tons. Her launch on 21st November 1934 was commemorated in lively journalistic style in the *Kirkintilloch Herald* of 28th November 1934:

> Kirkintilloch experienced all the thrills of the launch on Wednesday afternoon last, when the single-screw coasting steamer "Tuscan", built for Messrs J. Hay & Sons at their Kirkintilloch yard, was launched on the waters of the Forth & Clyde Canal. This was the second launch in a period of almost two years.
>
> A start was made with the vessel in July of this year, and, in order to have it completed for launching on the day fixed, it was found necessary for the yard employees to work overtime almost every evening during the past few weeks.
>
> A trim, sturdy coaster, she was the cynosure of thousands of eyes on Wednesday, for the fact that she was to be launched that day was known to almost everyone in the town. The launching was timed to take place at 2.15, but by 2 o'clock the various vantage points were literally black with spectators. The old wooden bridge would not have been able to stand the weight of the crowds which lined its sturdy successor.
>
> Among the crowds were children of one of the schools, who had been given leave of absence, under one of the teachers to see the launch, which was the first most of them had ever seen. The younger school children climbed onto the higher stretches of the opposite embankment, where a first-class view was afforded.
>
> In the presence of officials of the firm of Messrs J. Hay & Sons, the supports were knocked from beneath the steamer, and, to the accompaniment of a terrific roar from the spectatorate, the ship was launched broadside on. She took the water gracefully, a great flood of water swamping the canal walk for a

distance of about 50 yards. In several instances wet feet were the reward of those who had ventured too near.

The report well illustrates the impact of a launch from Hays' yard on the people of Kirkintilloch. It was a civic as well as an industrial event. *Tuscan* was engined by J. Hay & Sons Ltd., with a boiler by Muir & Findlay; but in 1948 she was converted to oil burning by McKie & Baxter, with a boiler from A. Anderson, Carfin. She foundered off Brodick on 7th June 1955. [85]

A new series of the smaller type of coasting boat was started in 1929 with the *Turk* (2), 70 gross tons. J. Hay & Sons Ltd. engined them up to 1936, after which McKie & Baxter took over. Boilers came from various sources; *Turk* (2) had hers from A. Marshall of Motherwell. She was with the Company until its final days, being broken up in 1964. [86] A fine silhouette of her appears as the frontispiece of Dan McDonald's book *The Clyde Puffer*.

The *Norman*, sold in 1930, was replaced in 1931 by the *Gael* (2), 70 gross tons, also engined by J. Hay & Sons Ltd., with her boiler by Marshall of Motherwell. Like the *Turk* (2) she was with the Company until its final days and was broken up in 1964. [87]

In 1931 *Briton* (4) was sunk. Her replacement was the *Slav*, 68 gross tons, launched in 1932 and engined at Port Dundas by J. Hay & Sons Ltd., with her boiler by Muir & Findlay of Glasgow. She was another that remained with the Company until the end. She was broken up in 1964. [88] The *Cuban*, 72 gross tons, was launched on 2nd December 1935. The *Kirkintilloch Herald* of Wednesday, 4th December 1935, described the event:

Messrs J. Hay & Sons Kirkintilloch yard was the scene of another fine launch — the second within a year — on Monday afternoon, when the trim single-screw coasting steamer "Cuban" went down broadside on to meet the waters of the canal.

In the presence of officials of the firm, the supports were knocked from beneath the steamer, and, at a given signal, the ropes were cut and to the accompaniment of a terrific cheer from the younger members of the spectatorate, the ship went down with great speed. As it took the water a great wave swamped the canal bank for a considerable distance.

The *Cuban* is said to have been given her name because John Hay had recently had a holiday in Cuba. She was the last new puffer to be engined by J. Hay & Sons Ltd. at Port Dundas. Muir & Findlay supplied her boiler. She worked for the Company until 1960, when she was broken up at Kirkintilloch.

These four — *Turk* (2), *Gael* (2), *Slav* and *Cuban* — were a little over 65 feet long. Later boats in the class had their length increased to 66.4 feet, with a slight increase in tonnage; otherwise they were similar to their predecessors. In these boats James Thom, who seems to have inherited much of his father's skill, brought Kirkintilloch puffers to their full stature. He may, however, have had some assistance with drawings made for him by Scott & Co. of Bowling. The boats had short raised quarterdecks, and the man at the wheel had some protection in the way of a dodger. During the Second World War all were equipped with wheel-houses of minimal proportions, except for the *Cuban*, whose burly skipper, Geordie Brown, had to have a specially large one built to accommodate his bulk. He was said to have had the wheel-house built around him.

January 1936 saw important changes at the yard. On Hogmanay 1935 George Thom was involved in a motor accident at Torrance Road End, near Kirkintilloch. He was taken to Glasgow Royal Infirmary with serious head injuries. He died there on 2nd January 1936, at the age of 69. His death was reported in the *Kirkintilloch Gazette* of Friday, 3rd January 1936. Two weeks later (17th January 1936) it reported the retiral of James Thom. For the first time since the start of the yard some seventy years before there was no member of the Thom family dealing with its daily running. Charles Meek took over the post of James Thom, with John Barrett assisting him. Barrett had been with the firm since 1916 and was well versed in the operations of the yard. They built four more of the smaller coasting boats: the *Texan*, 71 gross tons, in 1937; the *Inca*, 72 gross tons, in 1938; the *Cretan* (2), 72 gross tons, in 1939, and the *Boer*, 72 gross tons, in 1941. The names of the first three are said to have been inspired by John Hay's holiday travels. All four were engined by McKie & Baxter. *Texan* lasted until 1964, the others until 1965.[89] The *Inca* and the *Boer* made a name for themselves and enhanced the image of the puffer when they starred in the film "The Maggie". A Kirkintilloch man, Alexander Mackenzie, who had been a teacher in the Townhead School, played the part of the puffer skipper. Puffers from the yard at the Townhead Bridge seem to have had the

Boer off Dunoon on 5th October 1958.   *W. A. C. Smith.*

charisma required for film appearances — a quality developed unintentionally, perhaps, but a concomitant to their aesthetic appeal. The whole may be traced to the building by John Thom and the ability of his sons and their successors to carry it on.

In 1939 J. Hay & Sons Ltd. took their relationship with Scott & Co. of Bowling a step further when they went to them for two coasting boats larger than anything built at the Townhead yard and of a somewhat different design from the standard Kirkintilloch types. They were of 99 gross tons each and had wider counters and deeper cargo hatches than the boats built at Kirkintilloch. They were designed by Scott & Co. to the requirements of J. Hay & Sons Ltd. Drawings of them can be seen in the McLaren Collection of the Scottish Record Office, Western Archives, in the Adam Smith Building, Glasgow University. The boats, called *Anzac* and *Lascar*, were both launched in 1939. On the outbreak of war, the Ministry of War Transport took up their design and had a long series of ships built after it — 54 steam vessels and 9 diesels. They were classified by the letters VIC plus a number.[90] The Kirkintilloch yard was given orders for two of the steam vessels. *VIC 18* was launched in 1942 and after war service came back to J. Hay & Sons Ltd., who renamed her *Spartan* (3).[91] Today (1982) she is the only survivor of the Hay fleet. The other boat, launched in 1944, was not taken up as a VIC. She was made over to J. Hay & Sons Ltd., who named her *Kaffir*. In her original form she had a wheelhouse aft of the funnel and was a good example of the final development of the steam puffer. In spite of being based on a Scott design she managed to present something of the quality of the puffers of the Townhead Bridge yard. Later when she had been converted to diesel and had been altered in her superstructure, she lost most of that quality; but by way of compensation she joined the select company of Hays' puffer personalities in the film world when she featured in a production about the Loch Ness Monster. After thirty years of running for the Company and its successors, she was lost in December 1974.[92]

As in the previous World War, some of the Hay fleet were requisitioned for war service. Only three ships were built at the yard during the war period — the two VICs and the *Boer*. There was, however, plenty of overhauling, maintenance and repairing of small craft engaged in war work. The slip at Kirkintilloch was seldom empty: a variety of unfamiliar puffers and other craft occupied it. One boat, *VIC XI*, was so often at the yard's wharves or slip that the belief grew up in some quarters that she was a Kirkintilloch-built boat. This was strengthened at the end of the war when she was acquired by J. Hay & Sons Ltd. and renamed *Zulu*. In fact, she had been built at Goole.

After the war only one more boat was built in the yard. She was the *Chindit*, 74 gross tons, the final development of the smaller coasting type of boat. She is said to have been No. 62 in the yard's building list; but as the list has not been traced it is not clear how this number has been reached.[93] The launch of the *Chindit* was attended by a curious mishap. The *Kirkintilloch Herald* of Wednesday, 26th September 1945, reported it in some detail:

49

Chindit, the last puffer to be built on the Canal, seen here at Bowling.
G. E. Langmuir.

Close on one thousand spectators congregated on vantage points overlooking Messrs. J. Hay & Sons' canalside yard on Thursday afternoon received an entirely unlooked for thrill at the launching of the coastal steamer "Chindit". The snapping of an axe shaft brought about the mishap, resulting in the vessel being launched diagonally instead of broadside on, and the stern being embedded in the soft embankment at the water's edge. The accident occurred when the ropes were being cut prior to the launching. Following the accepted practice of the canalside launches, all supports were knocked away until only two stout ropes at bow and stern held the vessel in position. The simultaneous severing of the ropes allows the vessel to slip down to the water. So great is the strain imposed that one stout blow by each of the axe wielders is sufficient to sever the ropes. Unfortunately, as the workman at the stern struck his blow, the shaft of the axe snapped, and the rope was only partly severed. Meanwhile, rope No. 1 had been severed, and the bow slipped down to the water on the greased slipway and lay diagonally across the canal. To the accompaniment of much creaking and the splintering of wood the stern left the slipway and embedded itself in the soft embankment at the water's edge.

Workmen, seeking to free the stern, removed considerable quantities of earth and boulders. Later, the coaster "Caesar", lying west of the yard, was brought along, but all attempts to pull the "Chindit" from off the embankment failed. Heavy drenching showers made matters more difficult for the workmen and served to scatter the gallery of spectators, only a few remaining to witness the operations. The "Chindit" defied all efforts to move it off the embankment and still retained its diagonal position on Friday forenoon. The combined efforts of the workmen and the gallant little "Caesar" resulted in the "Chindit" being 100 per cent afloat shortly before midday.

This was the first mishap of its kind at the Kirkintilloch yard, all previous launches having been carried through with clockwork precision. The "Chindit" suffered little or no damage, and no person was injured. The "Chindit" is the 62nd coaster to be launched from the Kirkintilloch yard and the fourth since 1939. The three launches during the war years were "hush-hush" affairs, no publicity being permitted in accordance with war restrictions.

Almost all of Messrs. Hays' coasters have been named after ancient races. The "Chindit" is named after a tribe once dwelling at the foot of the Chindit Mountains in Burma. It measures 66 ft by 17 ft 6 in by 7 ft 9 in, and when complete will weigh 120 tons. A departure from precedent is the transfer aft of the skipper's cabin. The "Chindit" will be engined at Port Dundas and will afterwards be employed in the firm's near coasting trade.

The accident was an embarrassment to John Hay. It had been well photographed by the press. He bought all the negatives and prints to ensure that they were not published. There was a good deal of irony in such a completely unforeseeable accident at the final launching in a yard which had through long practice perfected the technique of launching broadside-on and which prided itself on its skill and efficiency in performing this operation.

The *Chindit* took her name from the name given to Orde Wingate's long-range raiders in Burma, who adopted as their badge the Chinthe, a mythological Burmese creature. The name was corrupted into 'Chindit'. There are no Chindit Mountains in Burma. It is interesting to note that the issue of the

Kirkintilloch Herald which reported the launch carried in another column a reference to a Kirkintilloch link with the Chindits:

> Corporal George Fyfe, elder son of Mr. and Mrs. Wm. Fyfe, Bridge-House, Kirkintilloch, has been awarded the Oak Leaf (mentioned in despatches) for making 27 consecutive flights over the Himalayas . . . in order to supply Wingate's raiders, "The Chindits", on their expedition into Burma.

It is unlikely that Corporal Fyfe would have flown over the Himalayas if he wanted to reach Wingate's Chindits; but he did have to fly over the Chin Hills, a hazardous operation which caused heavy losses in planes and men. To make 27 consecutive flights over them required stamina and skill as well as courage. Kirkintilloch had good cause to be proud of Corporal Fyfe.

After her flamboyant launch the *Chindit* settled down to steady work and gave the firm good service for 15 years. In the summer of 1960, after an overhaul at the yard, she was lying at Dunoon pier when, in the middle of the night, her wild Chindit spirit suddenly came to life again. She broke away from her moorings and bumped along the shore in the direction of Kirn, severely

General view of Hays' boatyard, from the Parish Church steeple.

damaging herself, and eventually came to rest on the shore very near the spot where, 81 years previously, James Hay's body had been found. In spite of sustaining damage which would have completely wrecked a less stoutly built ship, she was able to make her way to Kirkintilloch after being pulled off the beach. At Kirkintilloch she was slipped, but it was decided that she was too badly damaged to justify repair and she was sent to Bowling to be broken up.

In the aftermath of the Second World War economic conditions accentuated the decline in puffer trading which had begun in the inter-war years. The mounting cost of coal and oil and steadily rising wages made puffers increasingly uneconomical to run, particularly in competition with improved road transport. After a century of cheap fuel and low running costs, which made them a practical proposition, they began to be too expensive to justify their continuance. When J. Hay & Sons Ltd. built the *Chindit* they were fully aware that the building side of the yard would not continue. Although it was not immediately closed, its function was now repair work of various sorts. The wharfage provided moorings where some repairs could be done. Nine years later the old yard was finally dismantled. The *Glasgow Herald* of 5th June 1954 wrote:

> Kirkintilloch's well known canalside boatyard, the scene of many broadside launches, is no longer in use, and the employees of J. Hay & Sons, shipowners, Glasgow, have been transferring the gear to another of the firm's yards. The buildings in the old yard are being demolished.

The slip dock and its yard remained, its functions being limited to repairing, overhauling, dismantling and breaking up. About this time Charles Meek retired. John Barrett took over.

John Hay died in 1948 and for the first time in the history of the firm there was a short period when there was no member of the Hay family in charge. James McNab was Chairman. He had had long service with the firm on the coastal shipping side. Directors were John Urquhart, Charles Plews, James Downie and John Thom, who was Marine Superintendent of the coastal line. He was the son of George Thom. James Downie was in charge of the puffers and the maintenance and other work at the Kirkintilloch yard.

In 1950 J. M. Hay, son of William Hay, took over as Managing Director and the family connection was restored. His task in keeping the firm operational involved the closure of the old yard and concentrating the work on the slip dock. The Company still had 15 puffers and some horse-drawn scows, so that there was plenty of work for it. At the slipway an electrically driven winch had replaced the old steam engine and windlass. The engineering shop at Port Dundas had not made engines since 1936, when it engined the *Cuban*: but it continued to instal them and deal with minor machinery, with a gradually reducing work force.

After the Second World War dismantling and breaking up featured more prominently in the activities of the Kirkintilloch yard. In the 1940s the yard broke up four boats — *Victor* (1944), *Caesar* and *Tartar* (1947), *Hero* (1948). *Greek* and *Trojan* were both broken up in 1953, and *Celt* (2) was dismantled for use as a hulk. In 1956 *Moor* (2) suffered the same fate. *Cuban* was broken up in 1960. Most of the work was superintended by Charles Meek, who also in the 1950s organised the alterations required for the installation of radio telephones in the coasting boats. When John Barrett took over his main task was to keep the diminishing fleet maintained. He continued the tradition of the salvage and repair squad, which could go out to vessels of the Company requiring temporary repairs, and brought the squad to a high pitch of efficiency. He had started with the Company in the year of the launching of the first *Serb*. He was to see the last vessel go down the slipway — the *Slav* of 1932, after the last overhaul done at the yard. That event, however, was still some way off. John Barrett was in the best tradition of John Thom for good workmanship and ability to improvise. In his time the yard occasionally took in a fishing boat for repairs during its passage through the Canal.

In 1956 F. T. Everard & Co. took over the coasting line of J. Hay & Sons Ltd. To facilitate the changes involved, the puffers were separated from the ships of the coasting line by putting them into a company specially formed for the purpose, called the Cowal Coal and Trading Company. On 27th August 1956 J. Hay & Sons Ltd. transferred to the ownership of this company the puffers *Moor* (2), *Serb* (2), *Turk* (2), *Gael* (2), *Slav, Cuban, Texan, Inca, Cretan* (2), *Lascar, Anzac, Boer, Spartan* (3), *Kaffir, Chindit*. The name of the company was only a

Spartan (3), ex-*Vic* 18, under conversion to diesel at Kirkintilloch repair slip in June 1961.

John R. Hume.

title of convenience. On 11th December 1956 its name was changed to J. & J. Hay Ltd. and the puffers came under this title, as did the slip dock and the yard at Kirkintilloch. The Company acquired a Marine Superintendent, Hugh Alexander, who came from Burns, Laird & Co. He was responsible for the work on the puffers that went on at Kirkintilloch.

J. & J. Hay Ltd. (1956-1963)

The new Company was fighting a rearguard action. In 1959 it adopted the policy of converting its four best boats to diesel engines and phasing out the others for scrapping. This policy was carried out under the supervision of Hugh Alexander, in conjunction with Ajax Marine and Leyland Motors, for the installation of the diesels. *Lascar* and *Anzac* were converted in 1959, *Spartan* (3) in 1961 and *Kaffir* in 1962. By that time the closure of the Canal was imminent. The yard at Kirkintilloch had already been closed, although the wharf and engineering shop at Port Dundas were still in existence. The last job done at Kirkintilloch was a repair on the *Slav,* in November 1961. Her launch after repair, end-on into the slip dock, was the very last launch at the yard. The *Kirkintilloch Herald* on 1st November 1961 under the heading "Canalside boatyard is to close" had reported:

Kirkintilloch's canalside boatyard is to close on December 1. The men and apprentices employed on repair-work at the yard have had letters from Messrs. J. & J. Hay, shipowners and shipping merchants, 140 West George Street, Glasgow, informing them of the decision to close the yard.

"For a number of reasons we no longer find it possible to continue work at our boatyard" writes Mr. J. M. Hay, director, in a letter to the employees.

Regret is expressed at the necessity for such a step.

The men have been told that they will be guaranteed employment until December 1, but that they are free to leave at any time to seek new jobs.

A "Herald" reporter, who visited the yard on Monday, found workmen engaged on repair work to a Kirkintilloch-built puffer, "The Slav".

"That will probably be the last puffer to come to us for repair," said Mr John Barrett, foreman, who has been with the firm for 45 years.

The Kirkintilloch boatyard is about two years short of its century. At one time puffers for coastal trading were being turned out at about the rate of one per year.

The last puffer to be built at the Kirkintilloch yard was the "Chindit", launched just after the last war. Shortly afterwards the firm closed down the boatbuilding part of the yard and concentrated on repair work on the slipway yard further east. Small ships were pulled up the slipway and into the yard. . . .

In its peak years the Kirkintilloch yard employed thirty or more men. At the moment there are 11 men and three apprentices on the books.

The fact that the years of the Forth and Clyde Canal are numbered is thought to have some bearing on the firm's decision to close down their yard.

With its closing will pass one of Kirkintilloch's oldest industries.

Where the report spoke of 'the slipway yard further east' it should have said 'further west'.

The closure of the Canal, scheduled for 1st January 1963, made it impossible for the firm to operate from its traditional base; but it did not mean the complete extinction of the firm. In 1963 J. & J. Hay Ltd. joined with Hamilton & McPhail, also puffer owners, to form the firm of Hay, Hamilton Ltd. Most of the Hay boats were broken up in the next two years; *Turk* (2), *Gael* (2), *Slav* and *Texan* in 1964; *Inca, Boer* and *Cretan* (2) in 1965. The once bustling yard at Kirkintilloch presented a melancholy appearance. Much of it had already gone. The *Chindit* had been broken up in 1960. The *Kaffir* was lost in 1974. The sole survivor of a long line of puffers is the *Spartan* (3) which went to Glenlight Shipping on 19th August 1974, when Hay, Hamilton Ltd. joined with Ross & Marshall to form that Company. She ran for the Company until 1980, when she was withdrawn from service and moored in the basin at Bowling. The West of Scotland Boat Museum Association proposed that she should be preserved, as the nucleus of a maritime museum. They enlisted the help of the Royal Scottish Museum, Strathclyde Region and the Manpower Services Commission to have the old ship refurbished. Glenlight Shipping co-operated by donating her to the Museum. She was formally handed over at Bowling on 22nd June 1982. She now remains as one of the last representatives of a distinctive race of little ships which in their own quiet way made a fine contribution to Britain's maritime economy and which by their peculiar nautical personality endeared themselves to generations of Scots.

Of the places where the boats were built little traces remain. At Kirkintilloch the yards at the Townhead Bridge and at the Slip Dock have long since been completely dismantled. Part of the wharf at the Townhead Bridge can still be seen and among the bushes at the back of it are some masonry remains which are all that survive of the furnace. The Slip Dock has been left, with some of the wharfage, all very much overgrown and infested by the slimy green weed which seeks to choke the Canal everywhere. At Port Dundas nothing remains of the firm's yard and works. Fortunately, the importance of the Kirkintilloch yards as an integral part of the town's history has been appreciated and, thanks to the enthusiasm and energy of Mr. Don Martin, Reference Librarian at the William Patrick Library, a comprehensive collection of pictures of the yard and slip dock and of their products has been built up. Mr Martin has also recorded statements from men who worked in the yard and on the puffers and has put them into a valuable collection of 'memorabilia' about the history of the Canal at Kirkintilloch.

The contribution of the Hay family to the annals of British shipping extends far beyond the bounds of shipbulding; but in that particular sphere their achievements are impressive and unusual. They, more than any other group, developed the puffer in its design and functioning. Their workmanship was of consistently good quality. Their products were noted for their fine performance and endurance. They demonstrated the possibilities of inland shipbuilding, developing techniques and designs that were influential elsewhere. Their practice and experience produced what was perhaps the best type of steam lighter in its day. Their shrewdness and enterprise in the conduct of their varied business enabled them to survive the uncertainties of the shipping world, particularly in the shipbuilding part of it. Their policy of building in order to keep their work force occupied when there was no repairing or overhauling, and of selling or mortgaging vessels built in this way served them in good stead at times when other shipbuilders were feeling the pinch. They were a fine example of the ability of a well-run family business to bring prosperity and employment to its locality. William Hay, when he entered the business of boat-owning, laid a good foundation on which his sons, grandsons and great-grandsons were able to build. The little co-operative boatyard of Crawford & Co. afforded James and John Hay a potential for expansion which enhanced their business and brought a prosperity to Kirkintilloch and the Canal which entitles them to an honoured place in the records of both and justifies the belief expressed in the *Dumbarton Herald* of 18th June 1867, that 'this little co-operative venture should succeed'.

Peter McGregor & Sons (1902-1921)

For two decades at the beginning of the twentieth century Kirkintilloch had another shipyard, which contrasted strikingly with the Hays' yard in several respects. Peter McGregor was a timber merchant. His yard was developed as an adjunct to the timber trade and not, as in the case of the Hays, to meet the requirements of a shipping line. The Hays, with only a few exceptions, built solely for their own trade, with a policy of having one vessel on the stocks all the time to keep the work force occupied when there was no ship in for repairs or overhaul. Their yard was essentially a repair yard for their own vessels, with building a subsidiary function. McGregor, on the other hand, made building the sole function of his yard, taking orders from outside customers, some of them not even users of the Canal. The Hays concentrated on building puffers, with relatively little variation in dimensions and design, and all limited by the size of the Canal locks which they had to pass through. McGregor's vessels were of a variety of types, with tugs preponderating. They were not confined in their size to the limits of the Canal Locks. The yard used techniques already practiced at Kelvin Dock and Port Downie, of building vessels which were sent in sections for assembly outwith the Canal. The Hays had only one building berth, which was restricted by limitations of site and the fact that it gave directly onto the Canal. McGregor's yard, in the Railway Basin, had much more space for berths for launching and for fitting out. There were five building berths available, which helps to explain why McGregor, in a very much shorter period of existence than the Hays, was able to turn out twice as many vessels as they did: although as yard lists for neither firm have been traced, this popularly-accepted belief can be only an approximation. One thing which both firms had in common was the broadside launching of vessels. McGregor's yard, however, was better known outside the area of the Canal and the Firths of Clyde and Forth. It featured in Lloyd's lists of shipbuilders and was reported from time to time in journals dealing with shipbuilding matters. Generally speaking, it was a more sophisticated yard than that of the Hays.

Peter McGregor was born in Stirling about 1837. His parents moved to Kirkintilloch some time between 1843 and 1848. By 1861 they were both dead. Peter, their eldest son, was by then a wood merchant employing 12 men. He lived with his sister Janet and three brothers, James, John and William.[94] Peter had been in the timber business for several years. In 1858, at the age of 21, he had a sawmill at Oxgang and was applying to Joseph Cochran, of the Monklands Railways, for a lease of land at the Railway Basin on which to put a timber yard and a sawmill.[95] He was given the lease on a rent of £5 a year. He also obtained permission from the Canal Authorities to draw water from the Canal for a steam engine working his sawmill, and he was allowed an access road across the canal land on payment of £1 a year.[96]

Peter McGregor obtained his timber from Grangemouth, brought along the Canal. His trading areas included the West Highlands and Ireland. There is some reason to believe that he built some scows for his own use on the Canal. In 1874 he built a wooden smack of 54 gross tons for his trade in the west. She was called *Laburnum* and was the first recorded building in the Railway Basin. Reporting her launch, the *Dumbarton Herald* of Thursday, 19th November 1874, stated:

> On Thursday, shortly after 2 o'clock, there was launched from the boatbuilding yard of Mr Peter McGregor, a fine smart craft of 100 tons. There was a large assemblage of people present, when, as the vessel slipped away from the blocks, she was gracefully named the Laburnum, of Kirkintilloch, by Miss Mitchell, Westermoss. She will be ultimately employed in the timber trade, as Mr McGregor does a large business in that line along the West Highlands and Ireland. A considerable company of gentlemen adjourned to one of the workshops, which had been prepared for the purpose, and were handsomely regaled with cake and wine by the owners.

The fact that the report specifically mentions a boatbuilding yard suggests that there was something more than an 'ad hoc' arrangement for building the *Laburnum*. At the same time, it has been generally accepted that there was no other shipyard than that of the Hays at Kirkintilloch before 1902. The *Kirkintilloch Herald* of 6th December 1893, reporting the launch of the *Briton* from Hays' yard, quoted Captain Main as saying in a speech that this was the only yard Kirkintilloch could boast of. What probably happened at Peter McGregor's yard in the 1870s was that the carpenters, when necessary, built wooden scows for the company — or possibly for others — and had a particular place at the Basin where they did the building. This could have been the nucleus for the yard proper, when it came. Peter McGregor used the *Laburnum* until 1885, when he sold her to Rothesay traders. They sold her in 1919 to Irish owners. She was broken up in 1925.[97] McGregor also hired puffers and in 1891 bought from William Taylor of Grangemouth the iron screw puffer *Goliath*, 51 gross tons. He used her until 1920, when she was sold to the Tay. She was broken up in 1927. In 1892 McGregor acquired shares in the puffers *Seal* and *Walrus*, owned by J. M. Paton of Glasgow.[98] This experience of shipping, coupled with the fact that McGregor's son Peter had been serving an apprenticeship with Barclay, Curle & Co. on the Clyde, probably turned McGregor's thoughts to shipbuilding. He seems to have been friendly with the famous Thomas Seath of Rutherglen, who was a frequent visitor to the yard in its earliest days, before his death. Possibly Seath advised him about starting a shipyard. His relationship with McGregor may have been similar to that of Gilbert Wilkie with the Hays. At any rate, Peter McGregor, with his sons Peter and David, formed the company of P. McGregor & Sons and started building in their yard at the Canal Basin in 1902. The yard had a better site than had that of the Hays. There was much more room, and the proximity of the railway terminus with its sidings had certain advantages. Supplies of materials could be brought by train and dumped at the yard; and at a later stage ships built in sections could be sent by train to the point where they were to be assembled. An area on the southern extremity of the yard was used for building vessels which were to be sent off in sections by rail without launching. The railway company had a crane at the Basin which could be made available for fitting out vessels lying alongside the wharf where it was located.

Building berths at the Railway Basin yard of P. McGregor & Sons in 1912, with *Innisagra* ready for launching.

The yard was well equipped, with much more machinery than the yard of the Hays. The five building berths stood on the tongue of land between the two sections of the Basin. In the main workshop there was a 40hp Crossley gas engine which drove shafting, belts and pulleys for various items of plant — two punch, shearing and angle-cropping machines; 10-foot bending rolls; a straightening machine (called by the workmen 'squeezers'); a swing-jib counter-sinking drill; a vertical drilling machine; a 15-foot edge planing machine; a grindstone; an emery double-buffing wheel. This engine also worked the blower for the fires in the blacksmith's shop. The man in charge of this machinery and the Crossley engine was called Bob Burns. If he lacked the poetic fire of his great namesake, he kept the fires of industry going at the yard, attending also to the firing of the plate furnace, which was located in the shop.

The sawmill was located in another building, with the moulding loft above it. The loft was 200 feet long and 25 feet broad. Its large floor was painted black, to show up the lines of the vessels to be built, which were drawn in French chalk. The shape of frames and ribs was developed on a large blackboard. The sawmill below had its own power plant, a horizontal portable steam engine. There was no electrical power in the yard. The steam engine drove various woodworking machines, connected by a system of shafting, belts and pulleys, as in the main shed. The machines were: a 4-foot circular saw with a 2-foot moving table; a fixed 18-inch bench saw; a plank-logging saw with six vertical blades; a band saw. The engine was worked by a Highlander whose name has not been recorded. The head sawyer was called McCann. The band saw was attended to by James McIlhenny. There were three joiners — Peter Kerr, George Gardner, David Graham.

The horizontal engine supplied steam also to a steam hammer in the black-smith's shop. The head blacksmith, Jock Wardlaw, made his own tools — tongs, hammers, cold and hot chisels, flatteners, cresses and pullers. Using the steam hammer he forged stems, stern posts, propellor brackets, rudder posts, frames, pintles; handrail stanchions and hand railing; mountings for masts and derricks, towing hooks for tugs. He made also punches and blocks for punching machines, shear blades for shears and all drills. He worked in iron, mild steel or steel. There were three fires in the blacksmith's shop — one for Wardlaw, one for his assistant, Neil McKinnon and one spare, for anyone else needing a fire. Wardlaw was a man of outstanding skill and his work was an important contribution to the success of the yard's products. He was with Peter McGregor & Sons for the whole of their time. When the yard closed, J. Hay & Sons Ltd. were glad to take him onto their staff.

Of the shipwrights, four had their training under John Thom, at the Hays' yard — Donald Lang, James McGuigan, Robert Gray and his brother John, who joined the yard on his return from America. A fifth man, John Gordon, served his apprenticeship in McGregor's yard and stayed on as a shipwright.

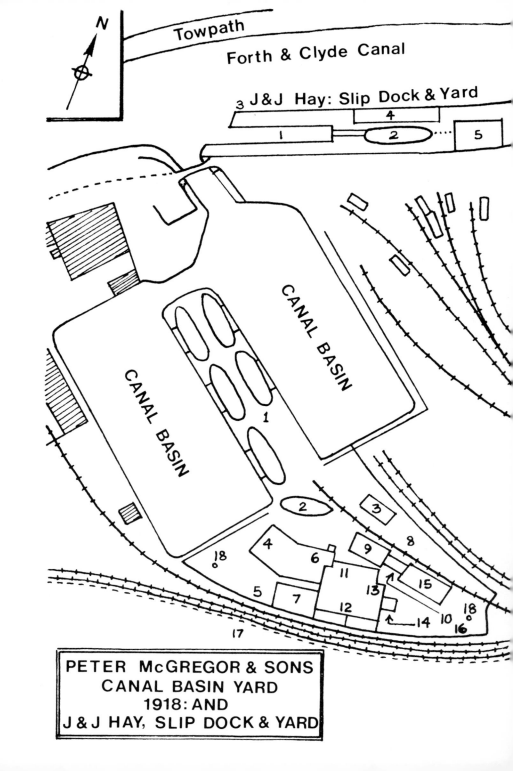

N

Towpath

Forth & Clyde Canal

3 J&J Hay: Slip Dock & Yard

4

1   2   5

CANAL BASIN

CANAL BASIN

CANAL BASIN

1

2   3

4   9   8

18   6

11   15

5   13

7   12   18

14   10   16

17

PETER McGREGOR & SONS
CANAL BASIN YARD
1918: AND
J & J HAY, SLIP DOCK & YARD

Peter McGregor & Sons
Canal Basin Yard

1   Five building berths.
2   Berth where 'MAY QUEEN' was built.
3   Offices.
4   Smithy.
5   Timber stack for sawmill.
6   Punching, planing and bending machinery.
7   Shearing and angle cropping machinery.
8   Sawn timber stacks.
9   Wood and template store.
10 Furnace for plates and angles.
11 Engine room — 'Crossley' gas engine.
12 Sawmill (moulding loft above).
13 Bolt and rivet shop.
14 Portable engine.
15 Blocks, board for frame shapes, paint store.
16 Sawn timber.
17 Area where vessels were built in sections for despatch by railway.
18 Cranes.

J. & J. Hay
Slip Dock and Yard

1   Slip Dock.
2   Slipway.
3   Wharf.
4   Shed for rivets and other parts.
5   Engine and windlass for slipway. Also punching and shearing machinery and foreman's office.

The platers were Donald McGillivray, James McGillivray and Tom Watson, with several apprentices working beside them. Henry McColl was the caulker, a skilled man who caulked seams and hand cut portholes, wash-port doors in bulwarks and coal-bunker scuttles. After some time a pneumatic hammer was brought in. It was worked by James Montgomery, who was the yard's first pneumatic caulker. McColl was retained to do jobs that required special skill.

In addition to the journeymen and craftsmen there were general labourers; and when necessary squads of riveters, hole-borers and platers came out from from Glasgow. Rivetting was done by hand in the early days, but in the closing years the yard had a pneumatic riveter. Two men, William McGeehan and Gilbert Blair, worked in the rivet, bolt and tool store. The paint store had a staff of two — one man in charge and another to help with the painting. Altogether the yard had a regular work force of about 50, which from time to time rose to as much as 100, according to the requirements of work.

A series of Foremen supervised operations in the yard. The first was called Cant. He was followed by James Burns, who had trained at McGregor's, gone on to John Brown's yard at Clydebank, and come back as McGregor's Foreman. When he left to go to Cammell, Laird's at Birkenhead, his place was taken by Donald McGillivray, promoted from his post as plater. The last Foreman was David Muil, who had been timekeeper and cashier in the office.

Peter McGregor Jr. was General Manager. He kept a close contact with his men, being for all practical purposes Yard Manager as well, working closely with the Foreman, and also with his brother David, who did administrative work in the yard office.[99]

The absence of yard lists and other records of the Company makes it impossible to obtain a full picture of the work of the yard; but from such information as is available it is possible to note certain salient features. The yard was a building yard: it had no special facilities for repairing and over-hauling. Vessels were launched broadside into the Canal Basin, except for the cruise steamer *May Queen*, which was launched end on. The dimensions of the vessels built were not limited by those of the Canal locks. Peter McGregor took orders for ships which had to be built in sections and sent elsewhere for assembly. Scotts at Bowling provided facilities for this; and some vessels were sent in sections by rail to other places, without having been launched. In order to help the men who did the assembling the hulls were painted red from the keel outward for the port side and green or black from the keel outward for the starboard. As a result, the yard was able to build a much wider range of types than the Townhead Bridge yard next door. Its specialty was tugs; but it built also puffers and small coasters, ferry boats, small oil tankers, small motor vessels and launches, both steam and motor. Most of the ships were single screw, but there were a few twin screw vessels. And, of course, there were barges, lighters and scows. The yard is said to have built 118 vessels in the two decades of its existence. The latest yard number so far traced is 115. P. McGregor & Sons had a wide range of foreign customers, particularly on the Continent, in South America and in the Middle East. Only a few of them registered their ships in Britain. Some of them are listed in Lloyd's Register or in the Mercantile Navy List, or appear in shipbuilding journals; but others left the yard without being recorded in this way. Some of them left without having been given a name, and where recorded had only their yard number. With the variety of customers, there was much less standardisation than at Hays' yard. Peter McGregor Jr. did any designing that was required.

The yard started with a series of large outside puffers for Coasting Steamships Ltd. The first of these was the steel screw steamer *Scout*, 97 gross tons, launched on 17th July 1902. The *Kirkintilloch Herald* of 23rd July 1902 reported:

Sergeant, built by P. McGregor & Sons in 1903 for Coasting Steamships Ltd., at Port Stewart, Northern Ireland.

Photo courtesy G. E. Langmuir.

From Messrs Macgregor's at the Canal Basin there was launched on Thursday a steel vessel of the largest dimensions possible to go through the canal locks. Her dimensions are 66ft by 18ft by 9½. As she left the ways she was christened 'Scout' by Miss Macgregor. The vessel is intended for canal and coasting traffic, and has been built for Glasgow owners. A cake and wine ceremony followed the launch, at which the owners of the new vessel were represented and the workmen afterwards were hospitably entertained. We understand a second vessel is to be laid down at once for the same owners.

The second vessel must have been on the stocks already, for she was launched on 30th November 1902, as reported in the *Kirkintilloch Herald* of 7th December 1902. She was named *Sentry* by Miss Park, of Ardeer, Lenzie. *Scout* and *Sentry*, 96 gross tons, were followed, in 1903, by *Sentinel*, 95 gross tons, and *Sergeant*, 96 gross tons. *Scout* and *Sentry* had single cylinder surface condensing engines of 25 NHP from Stewart & Mackenzie of Pollokshields. *Sentinel* and *Sergeant* had single cylinder inverted surface condensing engines of 17 NHP from McKie & Baxter of Govan. All had boilers from Richardson, Westgarth & Co. of Middlesborough. *Scout* was lost in the Corrievreckan Whirlpool on 7th July 1905. *Sentinel* was wrecked at Skinningrove in 1910. *Sentry* stranded on Achill Island in 1911 and became a total wreck. *Sergeant*, the sole survivor, was sold to Methil in 1912. [100]

The most interesting vessel to come from the yard in 1903 was the *May Queen*, 56 gross tons, for James Aitken, the Kirkintilloch man who ran cruises on the Canal between Port Dundas and Craigmarloch with the well-known 'Queens'. Her dimensions were 67.2ft. × 15.15ft. × 7ft.: press reports claimed that she was over 70 feet long, and so could not go through Canal locks, but was capable of being shortened if necessary. There seems to be no evidence to support this claim. The dimensions given here are from the Glasgow Port Registers. She had a 2-cylinder compound surface condensing engine of 22 NHP by Smith, Allan & Co. of Pollokshaws, with a boiler by J. Wallace & Co., Barrhead. The *Kirkintilloch Herald* of 20th May 1903 reported her launch:

There was successfully launched from the boatbuilding yard at the Basin, Kirkintilloch, of Messrs P. McGregor & Sons, on Wednesday afternoon, a sister boat to the present popular canal pleasure steamer, "Fairy Queen", and which is principally intended for cruise parties, picnics, Sabbath School trips, etc. The weather was fine, and the launch was witnessed by a good number of people, who lined the banks of the basin. The christening ceremony was successfully performed by Miss Ina Alexander, Fernlea, the boat as she left the ways being named "May Queen". The new steamer is similar in shape and appearance to the present "Fairy Queen", and it is expected that it will accommodate about 260 passengers. The cabins, decks, seatings, companions, etc., are of teak. There is also a bridge deck, with seats above and an awning over the whole. The cabins are tastefully done up, being upholstered all over with polished panelling of Kauri pine and teak. There is also cruise parties, purser's and captain's accommodation, while the tea cabin is large and roomy.

The steamer is to be fitted up with a complete installation of electric light. The engineers are Messrs. Smith and Allan, Pollokshaws, while Messrs. Walker Bros., Glasgow, are to put in the electric plant. The boat is expected to be ready for sailing by the end of the month.

The *May Queen* was the only one of James Aitken's boats to be built locally.[101] The *Kirkintilloch Herald* of 4th February 1903 had expressed the satisfaction of the town that the contract had gone to the new boatbuilding yard: '. . . It is gratifying to know that amongst the many offers sent in that of the local firm has been successful . . .' J. & J. Hay Ltd. had been invited to tender, but had too much work on hand to do so. The *May Queen*, under the designing of Peter McGregor Jr., had a yacht-like appearance, with a white hull and yellow funnel. Her predecessors, *Fairy Queens* (1) and (2), had red funnels with black tops. After the advent of the *May Queen*, *Fairy Queen* (2) adopted the yellow funnel, and this became the style for Aitken's steamers. *May Queen* ran on the Canal

Pleasure steamer *May Queen*, built by McGregor in 1903 at Kirkintilloch.

until the end of 1917, when she was sold to Palmer's Shipbuilding & Iron Co. Ltd., Hebburn-on-Tyne. In addition to being the only vessel to be launched from the yard stern first, she was the only steamer built there for purely pleasure cruising.

In its first full year of operation the yard was busy. The *Kirkintilloch Herald* of 21st October 1903, reporting the launch of the tug *Active*, 38 gross tons, on 17th October 1903, commented:

> This is the second launch within a fortnight from the same yard, and already the keel of another tug has been laid. The canal basin presents quite a harbour-like appearance just now, there being no fewer than five vessels there — the Fairy Queen, May Queen, Mr. Jas. Wallace's yacht, the Sergeant, launched a fortnight ago, and the Active, launched on Saturday.

In the next few years the yard built steamers for several foreign customers and made its first essays in building vessels which had to be sent elsewhere for assembly. Notable was the *Proyda*, a steel screw tug of 56 gross tons with a 2-cylinder surface condensing engine of 50 NHP, built for a firm in Odessa. Her launch on 20th January 1904 was reported in the *Kirkintilloch Herald* of Wednesday, 27th January 1904:

> Last Wednesday afternoon there was launched from the Basin boatbuilding yard of Messrs Peter McGregor & Sons, a steam tug built for a Russian Firm. Miss McGregor performed the christening ceremony, the tug being known as the "Proyda". A slight hitch occurred in the launching. The vessel being rather deep in the stern, she took the ground, and the assistance of a locomotive was necessary to get her afloat. Fortunately she sustained no damage. This firm are being fully employed, and have at present two boats in hand.

Two days later, J. & J. Hay Ltd. launched the *Roman*. The *Herald* drew attention to the fact that the launching of two boats in a week was a record in the history of shipbuilding at Kirkintilloch. When the building of both yards is combined, 1904 and 1905 may be considered to be the peak production years at Kirkintilloch. P. McGregor & Sons were proud of the *Proyda* and used her picture in one of their advertisements. It is interesting to note that, even at this late stage in steamship development, she was equipped with foresail and trysail.[102]

The year 1905 saw the firm's first essays in building ships for sectional assembly. The *Merlin* and the *Normand* were both well above the 100 gross tons mark. They appear in the firm's building list in Lloyd's Register; but no other information about them has been found. Other building in the year included the *Provencal* 15, 55 gross tons, the *Margaret*, 54 gross tons, and some small iron steam lighters whose names have not been traced. The tempo of building continued in 1906. The *Kirkintilloch Herald* of 2nd January 1907, reviewing shipbuilding for that year, stated:

> Peter McGregor, we learn from the Glasgow Herald Supplement, have launched five boats for Hull, Oporto, Calcutta, Buenos Aires and Cairo — total tonnage 300 tons.

Salvage tug *Proyda*, built by McGregor in 1903-4.

Only two of these five boats have been identified so far — the *Mars*, 47 gross tons, for Oporto, and the *Pioneer*, 50 gross tons, for W. Gillyot of Hull. The others are recorded by their yard numbers — No. 21, 60 gross tons; No. 27, 85 gross tons; No. 28, 55 gross tons. At least seven vessels were built in 1907, among them five steam tugs: the *Beaumont*, 58 gross tons, was launched for Stewart & Fulton of Glasgow, who sold her at once to Canada; the *Rayo*, 35 gross tons, went to Chile; the *Rosario*, 22 gross tons, and the *Manati*, 58 gross tons, went to Brazil. The *Manati*, whose launch was reported briefly in the *Kirkintilloch Herald* of 14th August 1907, was a tug for the Booth Line. She sailed from Kirkintilloch to Manaos, 2000 miles up the Amazon — a total distance of 6178 miles. The *Rosario*, much smaller, could not carry enough coal for the voyage to Brazil. She was rigged for sail and in spite of some hazards on the voyage crossed the Atlantic to Bahia safely. The fifth tug was the *Darfeel*, 92 tons, launched in August. She was built for owners in Alexandria, but never reached that port. The *Kirkintilloch Herald* of 18th December 1907 reported her wreck at Ras el Ghain. Fortunately, the crew were saved. The year 1908 continued the tempo of building — six screw tugs, one of them twin screw, including the *Teyr-el-Behr*, 64 gross tons, for the Egyptian Coastguard Administration, and the *Eider*, 31 gross tons, for the East India Distilleries and Sugar Factories, Madras. Another tug, No. 26, 49 gross tons, launched for Stewart & Fulton, went to a Quebec owner before the end of the year. Another feature of the yard's building at this period was steam launches. In 1908 it produced the *Suramento*, 10 gross tons, and in the following year the *Maya*, 15 gross tons. 1909 saw also the start of motor vessel production, with a small motor launch, the *Endrick*, 3 gross tons. Stewart & Fulton had another tug from the yard, the *Beauview*, 49 gross tons. She was with them for two years. On 24th June 1911 she left Gourock for Lisbon and disappeared without trace. In 1909, too, the Admiralty had a small tug, *Rosyth* No. 1, 26 gross tons, from the yard. [103]

One of the best known puffers to come from the yard was the *Ardfern*, 99 tons. She was launched in 1910 for T. Dougall and R. Stirrat of Glasgow. She had a long career, mainly on the Firth of Clyde, ending up with Warnock Brothers of Paisley, who ran her until 1966, when she was broken up at Dalmuir, after more than half a century of trading. [104]

For engines, McGregor & Sons went to various firms: Fisher & Co. of Paisley; McKie & Baxter of Govan; Gauldie & Gillespie and Houston & Co., of Glasgow. Boilers generally came from J. Wallace & Co., Barrhead, or A. & W. Dalgleish, Glasgow.

In 1911 the yard launched the *Torias*, 70 tons, for a French firm, and some motor launches for the colonies. There was also a twin screw steel vessel of 85 gross tons which has not been named in records available. She carried the yard number 50.

In 1912 P. McGregor & Sons came before the public eye by their participation in an experiment with motor coasting vessels. As the internal combustion engine developed in the early 1900s there was a good deal of interest in its possibilities as a means of propulsion for ships, and various experiments were made, particularly in Russia, where some motor gun boats were produced for patrols in the Black Sea and elsewhere. John M. Paton, of Paton & Hendry's Glasgow Steam Coasters, believed that it had potential for powering small motor coasters of the puffer type, or slightly larger. [105] He formed the Coasting Motor Shipping Company in Glasgow and gave orders for eighteen motor coasters. Eight of the orders went to Peter McGregor & Sons; six were for boats with dimensions of conventional steam puffers, which they resembled in appearance except that they lacked funnels and had an overhanging counter with the exhaust from the engine coming out below it. They had a 16-foot quarterdeck with a deck house at the fore end. On top of the deck house were the wheel, binnacle and engine-room telegraph — a novelty not found in steam puffers of the day. The other two boats were slightly larger in their dimensions, but were similar in general features. All the boats had names beginning with *Innis*. . . .

As the boats came off the stocks and ran their trials they attracted a good deal of attention. *Innisagra, Innisbeg, Inniscroone* and *Innisdhu* were launched in 1912; *Inniseane* and *Innisfree* in 1913. [106] Their tonnage was 94 to 95 gross. They were in the smaller class, described as the first 'motor puffers'. They were reported in the press and were written up in shipbuilding and engineering journals, and their performances were watched with interest. As they were to some extent experimental, various types of engine were tried out in them. *Innisagra, Inniscroone* and *Innisdhu* had 2-cylinder vertical 2-stroke 'hot-bulb' engines giving 80bhp by J. & C. G. Bolinder of Stockholm. *Innisbeg* had a

Model of the *Innisbeg*. one of the McGregor-built 'motor puffers' for J. M. Paton's Coasting Motor Shipping Company.

direct acting 2-cylinder engine of 80NHP by William Beardmore & Co., Dalmuir. *Inniseane* and *Innisfree* had Kromhout Marine Engines by D. Goedhoop, Amsterdam, generating 110 ihp. The working of these engines was watched with care and interest and was discussed in comparison both with conventional steam engines and with each other. The two larger boats, *Innisclora* and *Innishowen*, which came out in 1913, were of 117 and 118 register tons respectively.[107] Their dimensions of 74.7ft. × 18.3ft. × 8.7ft. made them too large to go through the Canal locks. Accordingly, the bow section up to the forward bulkhead was left unrivetted and was dismantled and stowed in the hold when the vessels were sent to Bowling for assembly. Men from McGregor's yard went down to Bowling and put the ships together on one of the slips at Scott's yard. These two larger vessels were each powered by a 2-

cylinder Kromhout 'hot bulb' engine. Mr J. McCash, a former employee of P. McGregor & Sons, has given an interesting description of the process of starting the 'hot bulb' engine:

> There was a dome or bulb on top of each cylinder. These were pre-heated with a paraffin blow lamp, one at each cylinder head. A compressed air cylinder was pumped by a hand-operated inflator to 14 to 18 atmospheres. The fly wheel was turned to just over dead centre with a crow-bar inserted into holes in the rim. The bulbs grew red hot. You pulled the throttle lever, the compressed air turned the engine over, the oil fired the cylinder, and the engine started to thump. A small compressor attached to the engine refilled the air bottle. The exhaust came out under the counter — there was no funnel.[108]

The publicity given to McGregor's 'Innis' boats has given an impression that they were something unique, a pioneering venture in motor vessels. Apart from the fact that other 'Innis' boats were being built at Alloa and Leith, it should be noted that in 1912 the Greenock and Grangemouth Dockyard Company at Grangemouth launched for James Rankine's canal and estuarial trade a motor lighter called the *Peggy,* of dimensions and tonnage very similar to those of the smaller 'Innis' boats, and powered by a Kromhout engine. Her claim to the title of 'first motor puffer' is probably as good as that of the 'Innis' boats. The 'Innis' boats were not a success. The new type of machinery caused trouble and breakdowns, largely through the inexperience of the operators. The outbreak of the First World War prevented the boats from being given a long enough trial to iron out these problems, so that the boats never had a fair chance of showing what they could do. The *Inniseane* foundered off Port Ellen, Islay, on 19th September 1914 and the *Innisfree* went to the Admiralty in 1916. The *Inniscroone* and the *Innisbeg* were sold to Hull in 1918: the *Inniscroone* was renamed *Truro Trader* in the mid-20s. The *Innisclora* went to the Russian Government in 1923. The *Innishowen* went to John Summers & Co., Shotton, about the same time. She was lengthened and re-engined. In 1947 she went to Denmark as the *Eva Petersen*. The *Innisagra* was sold after the war and ended up in Sierra Leone in 1930, where she was converted into a barge. The *Innisdhu* was sold also. Renamed *Ben Olliver,* she was sunk in the Thames after an explosion on 20th September 1940.[109]

Although the main products of the yard in 1912 and 1913 were the motor coasters, other vessels were turned out also, including the *North Star,* a tug of 35 gross tons for the North Russian Trading Company, launched in 1912; and another tug, No. 69, 53 gross tons, in the following year; and, of course, there were some barges. The oil engine, however, continued to feature in the yard's building. During the First World War the yard built a number of 30-foot turtle-decked pinnaces, each fitted with a towing hook, for use at the beaches in the Dardanelles campaign. They were powered by single-cylinder Bolinder engines. They were given their trials on the Canal and then were brought in to the wharf in the Basin where the railway crane lifted them onto flat cars to go to the docks at Glasgow for transhipment. The yard also built some 120-foot square-ended dumb barges for work on the Tigris during the campaign in Mesopotamia.

These barges were split amidships after launching, the two halves being towed down to Bowling and out into the Clyde, where they were towed up to the large crane at Cessnock, reassembled by men from McGregor's yard and loaded onto cargo ships for transport to the Middle East.

In 1915 the twin-screw tug *Thegon* was built for the Petroleum Steamship Company Ltd. With a tonnage of 174 gross, she had to be sent in sections to Greenock, where she was assembled and given her 4-cylinder diesel engine by J. G. Kincaid & Co. In the next year the yard launched the *Perfection*, a motor puffer of 73 gross tons with a 2-stroke single acting internal combustion engine by William Beardmore & Co. She was owned by the Anglo-American Oil Co. and ran on the Canal for many years. She was sold to the Admiralty in 1957.

Starfinch, built by McGregor in 1921.   *Dan McDonald.*

She was of unusual design, having two large square tanks, each with three compartments, so that she could carry several different types of cargo at the same time.[110]

Just before the start of the First World War in 1914 the yard launched a small twin-screw ferryboat for Sunderland Corporation. She was called *Sir Walter Raine* and was the subject of an amusing incident at her trials. When she was being fitted out, the task of connecting up the hand steering gear was given to Jack McCash, one of the younger men, at that time inexperienced in the work. In connecting the chains with the wheel he omitted to cross them, as is required for a proper response to a turn of the wheel. When the wheel was tested while the steamer was lying in the Basin it worked very smoothly; but when she was drawing out of the Basin to start her trial and the helmsman put over the wheel to turn her to starboard, she turned to port and ran into the quay wall. McCash survived.[111]

The immediate post-war years were difficult ones and in spite of several orders the firm found it hard to keep going. Peter McGregor Jr. was in charge now, and he felt that the struggle was not worthwhile. In 1920 two small tugs for the Admiralty were launched, the *Buckie Burn* and the *Rathven Burn*. Four larger steamers, after the style of puffers, were built to the order of E. H. Bennett & Co., Newport, Monmouthshire — *Benfinch* and *Kenfinch* in 1920, *Starfinch* and *Rockfinch* in 1921. None of them remained very long with Bennett & Co.; *Rockfinch*, in fact, was sold at the Basin yard to a West Indian owner and sailed for Demerara on 8th July 1921. She arrived safely several weeks later. *Kenfinch* went to T. Rigby & Sons, Liverpool. *Benfinch* was sold to W. B. Ritchie of Fraserburgh and foundered eight miles off the Mull of Kintyre on 3rd September 1922. *Starfinch* had several changes of owner and was back in the Clyde before a year was out. She was bought by J. Hay & Sons Ltd. in 1950. On 18th December 1952, on a voyage from Tobermory to Castlebay with coal, she was abandoned in heavy weather fifteen miles east of Heisker. She was taken in tow, but sank off Ardnamurchan on 19th December. The tow crew were saved.

Another steamer similar in all respects to the four 'Finch' boats was the *Wynor*, owned by John Stewart of Glasgow. She was launched in 1921, but had a short life, foundering in the Moray Firth on 21st February 1923.[112] These were the last ships to be built at the yard. It closed in 1921 and was dismantled. Today, in the 1980s, no trace of it remains. The Railway Basin has been filled in and built over. The railway yard has long since been taken up. Even the Canal has ceased to infiltrate its waters at the old entrance to the Basin. Peter McGregor & Sons had a relatively short life compared to their neighbours, the Hays; but in that life they built some good ships and greatly enhanced the reputation of Kirkintilloch as an inland shipbuilding centre. The two shipbuilding firms at Kirkintilloch complemented each other and between them provided a pattern of building that was varied and versatile. Together they built up a tradition of shipbuilding which has made Kirkintilloch unique in the Scottish shipbuilding world.

REFERENCES

BR/FCN	British Rail: Forth & Clyde Navigation Papers.
BWB	British Waterways Board, Offices at Old Basin, Applecross Street, Hamiltonhill, Glasgow.
GPR	Glasgow Port Registers.
Mins.	Minutes of Meeting of Directors, J. & J. Hay Ltd.
MNL	Mercantile Navy List.
SRO(NRH)	Scottish Record Office, New Register House.
SRO(WRH)	Scottish Record Office, West Register House.

1. Greenock Port Registers 1786 — *Jean and Janet.*
2. SRO(WRH): BR/FCN/1/11 — Minutes of Committee of Management, 6th March 1783 and 17th April 1783.
3. *Ibid.*
4. SRO(WRH): Information about the provision of these yards can be found in the records of the Forth & Clyde Navigation (BR/FCN/—).
5. SRO(WRH): BR/FCN/1/20 — Minutes of Council, 18th December 1829.
6. In the 1880s Samuel Crawford was Yard Manager with Messrs. J. & G. Thomson, Clydebank. (H. D. Brown, *Clydebank Shipyard,* 1954. Clydebank Public Library.) In 1886 he became one of the first Commissioners of the new Police Burgh of Clydebank (*Lennox Herald,* 15th January, 18th and 25th June and 29th October 1887). In 1892 he went to Kinghorn, Fife, as a partner in the Abden Shipyard of John Scott & Co. Ltd. (*Dumbarton Herald,* 15th June and 14th September 1892). He died in Liverpool in 1903.
7. The tradition that the *Ceres* was built at Kirkintilloch about 1865 is a very strong one, and so cannot be entirely ignored. Mr. J. M. Hay has suggested that she could have been built on the Canal bank *before* the start of the yard at Townhead Bridge, and that her building may have been a factor in the decision to start a yard. Mr. Hay has suggested that John Thom may have been her builder, and has pointed out that he is looked on as the father of shipbuilding at Kirkintilloch. Unfortunately, no evidence to support this theory has been found. The Glasgow Port Registers (Vol. 21 (1886-88) — *Ceres*) state that she was built by J. & J. Hay in 1875 at Kirkintilloch. Mr. Hay has suggested that this could refer to a re-building of the hull and the engining of it, as was done with the *Hercules* in 1878, at Hamiltonhill, with material from an earlier *Hercules,* built at Kelvin Dock in 1869. The whole matter is uncertain; but it can be accepted that Crawford & Co.'s yard is the first of which there is any evidence at Kirkintilloch, and that it was started in the autumn of 1866.
8. BWB: Forth & Clyde Navigation Titles, Bundle No. 308 — Report as to Supply of Water from the Forth & Clyde Canal, from 1828.
9. William Hay appears in the Kirkintilloch Voters' Rolls of 1842 as 'farmer' and in those of 1844 as 'boatman'. In the Kirkintilloch Census Register of 1841 he is shown as 'Farmer at Hillhead'; in that of 1851 as 'Boatmaster at Hillhead'; in that of 1861 as 'Farmer of 166 acres at Hillhead'; and in that of 1871 as 'Retired Farmer and Boatowner'. (SRO(NRH): CEN 1841/1851/1861/1871/498).
10. James Hay appears in the Kirkintilloch Census Register of 1851 as 'Boatmaster', but does not appear in subsequent Kirkintilloch Census Registers. The Post Office Directories of Glasgow show that he had moved into the City in 1857 and was conducting a shipping and forwarding agent's business at Port Dundas.
11. *Glasgow Herald,* 5th July 1862.

12. SRO(NRH): CEN 1861/498, Block 6. John Hay described himself as 'Farmer's son'.
13. GPR Vol. 18 (1881-83) — *Alfred.*
14. A copy of the Agreement, made available by courtesy of Mr. J. M. Hay, may be seen in the William Patrick Library, Kirkintilloch.
15. GPR Vol. 9 (1869-71) — *Helena.*
16. *Ibid.* and Vol. 21 (1886-88) — *Louise.*
    Helena — 42 gross tons. 64.3ft × 14.45ft × 5.7ft. 10hp.
    Louise — 43 gross tons. 65.2ft × 14.3ft × 5.5ft. 15hp.
17. A copy of this Agreement of 1867, made when the Caledonian Railway Company became the Proprietors of the Forth & Clyde Canal, is available in the William Patrick Library, Kirkintilloch, by courtesy of Mr. J. M. Hay.
18. GPR Vol. 12 (1872-73) — *Lizzie Gardner.*
19. GPR Vol. 21 (1886-88) — *Leopold.*
20. GPR Vol. 28 (1895-96) — *Beatrice;* Vol. 29 (1896-97) — *Alice.*
21. GPR Vol. 28 (1895-96) — *Vulcan;* Vol. 29 (1896-97) — *Hero* and *Victor.*
22. Mins. 27th April 1915, 26th May 1915, 26th June 1915.
23. GPR Vol. 21 (1886-88) — *Ceres.*
24. GPR Vol. 3 (1859-61) and Vol. 18 (1881-83) — *Agnes.*
25. GPR Vol. 14 (1875-76) — *Adelaide.* and Vol. 21 (1886-88) — *Arthur.*
26. Most of this information about the yard has been supplied by courtesy of Mr. James MacKinnon, a former employee at the yard.
27. J. Horne, ed., *Kirkintilloch* (1910), p. 183.
28. The fatality was reported in the *Glasgow Herald* of 13th August 1879.
29. Information about the term 'shorehead boats' supplied by courtesy of Mr. J. M. Hay. Further information on this subject and connected matters is to be found in a note by Mr. Hay in the William Patrick Library, Kirkintilloch.
30. Letter of Mr. J. M. Hay to the writer, 12th June 1982.
31. Mr. J. M. Hay has pointed out this pattern of naming in James Hay's screw lighters.
32. GPR Vol. 18 (1881-83) — *Leo.*
33. GPR Vol. 21 (1886-88) and MNL 1891 — *Dinah.*
34. GPR Vol. 24 (1890-92) — *Craigielea;* and Transcripts of the Shipping Register belonging to Messrs. Thomas McLaren & Co. (Glasgow) Ltd., in Strathclyde Regional Archives (ref. AGN 458).
35. GPR Vol. 24 (1890-92) — *Amy; Kirkintilloch Herald,* 20th May 1896; Mins. 24th February 1899.
36. GPR Vol. 21 (1886-88) — *Albert.*
37. *Ibid.* — *Scotia.*
38. Letters of J. & J. Hay to Mr. Jas. H. Clapperton, Port Dundas, 18th July 1888 and 4th August 1888, in William Patrick Library, Kirkintilloch.
39. Letter of Caledonian Railway Co. to Messrs J. & J. Hay, 30th July 1888, in William Patrick Library, Kirkintilloch.
40. Information by courtesy of Mr. J. M. Hay, Mr. J. MacKinnon and Mr. J. McCash.
41. GPR Vol. 25 (1892-93) — *Orion.*
42. *Ibid.* — *Argo.*
43. Mins. 1898 and 1899 — *Neptune* and *Nelson.*
44. GPR Vol. 26 (1893-94) — *Nelson.*
45. *Ibid.* — *Briton.*
46. GPR Vol. 27 (1894-96) — *Celt,* and Mins. 25th January 1905 and 22nd February 1905.
47. Mins. 18th April 1902.
48. GPR Vol. 27 (1894-96) and Vol. 37 (1906-07) — *Saxon;* Mins. 18th April 1902, 25th September 1906, 28th June 1907; and Annual Report of Directors, J. & J. Hay Ltd., for 1906.

49. Mins. 22nd July 1902 and *Kirkintilloch Herald,* 3rd September 1902.
50. Mins. 27th April 1915, 26th May 1915 and 26th June 1915.
51. GPR Vol. 28 (1895-96) — *Norman,* and Mins. 30th December 1912, 28th January 1913, 25th September 1914.
52. GPR Vol. 28 (1895-96) — *Briton,* and Vol. 29 (1896-97) — *Gael.*
53. Mins. 28th December 1897, 27th October 1899, 28th February 1906, 22nd May 1906, 27th August 1906 and 26th April 1909.
54. Prospectus of J. & J. Hay Ltd. A copy is available in the William Patrick Library, Kirkintilloch, by courtesy of Mr. J. M. Hay.
55. *Ibid.*
56. Mins. 30th November 1898 (erroneously entered '1899' in Minute Book).
57. GPR Vol. 29 (1896-97) — *Tartar;* Vol. 31 (1898-1900) — *Druid;* Vol. 32 (1900-01) — *Moor.*
58. Mins. 27th December 1898.
59. Mins. 2nd May 1899.
60. Mins. 24th February 1899 and 29th December 1899.
61. GPR Vol. 30 (1897-98) and Vol. 35 (1904-05) — *Dane.*
62. GPR Vol. 32 (1900-01) — *Turk.*
63. GPR Vol. 31 (1898-1900) — *Druid;* Mins. 28th August 1905.
64. Mins. 23rd August 1898 and 24th August 1899 — *Lookout.*
65. GPR Vol. 25 (1892-93) — *Roslin Glen;* Vol. 32 (1900-01) — *Macnab;* Vol. 34 (1903-04) — *Dorothy.*
66. Mins. 23rd August 1900 and 28th September 1900.
67. Mins. 3rd November 1896 and 2nd September 1897; and Annual Report of Directors, J. & J. Hay Ltd., for 1902.
68. GPR Vol. 41 (1911-12) — *Gascon;* Vol. 43 (1913-14) and Vol. 49 (1924-27) — *Saxon (ex Dane).*
69. Mins. 28th April 1913 and 15th May 1913.
70. Mins. 20th December 1904, 25th January 1905 and 22nd February 1905.
71. GPR Vol. 35 (1904-05) — *Briton,* Mins. 25th September 1914.
72. GPR Vol. 36 (1905-06) — *Trojan.*
73. GPR Vol. 36 (1905-06) — *Druid;* Mins. 25th July 1912, 22nd August 1912, 30th August 1915, 24th September 1915, 28th May 1919.
74. Mins. 19th March 1906, 22nd May 1906, 27th August 1906 and 15th January 1907.
75. GPR Vol. 37 (1906-07) — *Celt;* Mins. 29th January 1915 and 25th February 1919.
76. Mins. 31st August 1914 and 21st April 1919 and GPR Vol. 38 (1907-08) — *Cossack;* and Vol. 40 (1909-11) — *Cretan.*
77. GPR Vol. 44 (1914-16) — *Serb;* Mins. 25th February 1916, 13th March 1916, 23rd June 1916 and 22nd December 1916.
78. Mins. 26th July 1910.
79. Mins. 26th January 1912 and 29th February 1912.
80. Mins. 23rd June 1916 and 27th July 1916.
81. Mins. of 1917 and 1918.
82. Information by courtesy of Mr. C. M. Ross, formerly of J. Hay & Sons Ltd.
83. GPR Vol. 48 (1920-24) — *Moor.*
84. GPR Vol. 49 (1924-27) — *Serb.*
85. GPR Vol. 51 (1931-36) — *Tuscan.*
86. GPR Vol. 50 (1928-30) — *Turk.*
87. GPR Vol. 51 (1931-36) — *Gael.*
88. *Ibid.* — *Slav.*
89. GPR Vol. 52 (1937-40) — *Texan, Inca, Cretan* (2); Vol. 53 (1941-45) — *Boer.*
90. VIC — Victualling Inshore Craft. There is also a suggestion of VICtory.
91. In 1901 J. & J. Hay Ltd. bought the *Macnab.* 89 gross tons, from W. H. King and renamed her

Spartan. She was sold in 1923. In 1926 they bought the *Tiree*, 92 gross tons, from C. & J. Lamont of Tiree. She was renamed *Spartan* (2). During the war she was requisitioned by the Government. While still on Government service she blew up and sank off Lismore on 31st May 1946. *Vic* 18 was made over to J. Hay & Sons Ltd. by way of replacement. Her name was changed to *Spartan* on 24th September 1946 — the third ship in the fleet to bear the name. (GPR Vol. 32 (1900-01) — *Spartan* ex-*Macnab*; Vol. 37 (1906-07) — *Spartan* ex-*Tiree*; Vol. 53 (1941-45) — *Spartan* ex-*Vic* 18.)

92. GPR Vol. 53 (1941-45) — *Kaffir*.
93. Yard numbers quoted by the press do not always tally with known numbers of building and should be treated with caution.
94. SRO(NRH): CEN 1861/498, Block 12.
95. P. McGregor to Joseph Cochran, 19th October 1858; Card No. P1123 in records at William Patrick Library, Kirkintilloch.
96. BWB: Forth & Clyde Navigation Titles, Bundle No 308 — Report as to Supply of Water from the Forth & Clyde Canal, from 1828; and Ledger of Rents & Feu Duties, 1884-1928.
97. GPR Vol. 13 (1874-75) — *Laburnum*.
98. GPR Vol. 16 (1878-79) — *Goliath*; Vol. 25 (1892-93) — entries for *Seal* and *Walrus*.
99. Information about plant and personnel by courtesy of Mr. J. McCash, a former employee at the yard.

100. GPR Vol. 33 (1901-02) — *Scout*; Vol. 34 (1902-03) — *Sentry, Sentinel, Sergeant*.
101. GPR Vol. 34 (1902-03) — *May Queen*.
102. *Ibid.* — *Proyda*.
103. GPR Vol. 37 (1906-07) — *Mars, Beaumont*; Vol. 38 (1907-08) — No. 26; Vol. 39 (1908-09) — *Beauview*. Lloyd's Register, 1911-12 — *Rayo, Rosario, Manati, Eider*; 1912-13 — *Teyr-el-Behr*; 1922-23 — *Provencal* 15, *Rosyth* No. 1.
104. GPR Vol. 40 (1909-11) — *Ardfern*.
105. This was the John Muir Paton in whose boats *Seal* and *Walrus* Peter McGregor took shares in 1892.
106. *The Shipping World*, Vol. XLVI (Jan.-June 1912): *Innisagra*, Launched 1st May 1912; *Innisbeg*, launched 31st May 1912; *Inniscroone*, launched 11th June 1912.
    Ibid., Vol. XLVII (July-Dec. 1912): *Innisdhu*, launched 25th September 1912.
    Ibid., Vol. XLVIII (Jan.-June 1913): *Inniseane*, launched 21st February 1913; *Innisfree*, launched 3rd April 1913.
107. *Shipbuilding & Shipping Record*, 3rd July 1913-4th September 1913: *Innisclora*, launched 26th June 1913 and *Innishowen*, launched 30th August 1913. Also GPR Vol. 43 (1913-14).
108. *P. McGregor & Sons* — Account by Mr. J. McCash, quoted with his permission. In William Patrick Library, Kirkintilloch.
109. GPR Vol. 41 (1911-12) — *Innisagra*; Vol. 42 (1912-13) — *Inniscroone, Innisbeg, Innisdhu, Inniseane, Innisfree. Inniscroone* renamed *Truro Trader* (Lloyd's Register, 1926-27).
110. GPR Vol. 44 (1914-16) — *Perfection*; Lloyd's Register, 1926-27 — *Thegon*.
111. Anecdote by courtesy of Mr. J. McCash, Kirkintilloch.
112. GPR Vol. 46 (1920-22) and Lloyd's Register, 1926-27 — *Wynor*; Lloyd's Register, 1922-23 — *Buckie Burn, Rathven Burn, Benfinch, Kenfinch, Starfinch, Rockfinch*.

ACKNOWLEDGEMENTS

I am most grateful to Mr. J. M. Hay, late of J. Hay & Sons Ltd. and J. & J. Hay Ltd., for his kindness in making available papers of J. & J. Hay Ltd. and other records from his collection of the firm's documents, and for his advice and information on many matters relating to the ships and shipbuilding of Kirkintilloch, which have been invaluable in preparing this account. I should like to express my thanks for all that he has done to further that preparation.

I should like to thank also the following ladies and gentlemen who have given helpful assistance in the gathering of material for this account:

Mr. C. M. Ross, Milngavie
Mr. R. N. W. Smith, Radernie, Fife
Mr. J. MacKinnon, Kirkintilloch
Mr. J. McCash, Kirkintilloch
Mr. G. E. Langmuir, Bearsden
Mr. A. Crawford, Dalmuir
Mr. J. Robertson, Glasgow
Mr. W. Lind, Bridge of Weir.
Mr. D. Burrell, Sevenoaks, Kent
Mr. H. Gillies and Mrs. A. M. Searson, Portcullis House, Glasgow
Mr. D. C. Cameron, British Waterways Board, Hamiltonhill
Miss S. Buchanan and Mr. D. Cameron, Clydebank Museum
Mr. M. Taylor, Dumbarton Public Library.

I should like to thank the following gentlemen for permission to reproduce photographs:

Mr. J. M. Hay
Mr. D. McDonald
Mr. G. E. Langmuir
Mr. C. M. Ross
Mr. J. R. Hume.

And finally, I should like to thank particularly Mr. D. Martin, William Patrick Library, Kirkintilloch, who initiated this project and has sustained it with his advice and help.

VESSELS BUILT AT TOWNHEAD BRIDGE YARD

Year	Name	O.N.	Type	Tons	Dimensions	Engine	Owner
			CRAWFORD & CO.				
1867	Rainbow		Composite Lighter	100 bdn	62.0 × 16.5 × 8.00		Colthorpe & Dewar, Dumbarton
			J. & J. HAY				
1869	Helena	60441	Iron Screw	42 gross	64.3 × 14.45 × 5.70	10hp 1-cyl.	J. & J. Hay
1872	Hugh		Iron Lighter	85 bdn			J. & J. Hay
1872			Iron Lighter				
1873			Iron Lighter				
1873	Lizzie Gardner	68065	Iron Screw	75 gross	65.8 × 18.60 × 8.60	20hp 2-cyl.	J. Gardner & Sons, Kirkintilloch
1875	Leopold	93364	Iron Screw	35 gross	66.0 × 13.20 × 4.80	10hp 1-cyl.	J. & J. Hay
1875	*Ceres	93365	Iron Screw	38 gross	65.0 × 13.70 × 4.60	12hp 1-cyl.	J. & J. Hay
1876	Adelaide (2)	76722	Iron Screw	58 gross	65.4 × 17.70 × 7.50	10hp 2-cyl.	J. & J. Hay
1877	Arthur	95020	Iron Screw	52 gross	65.7 × 16.20 × 5.90	10hp 1-cyl.	J. & J. Hay
1880	Lyra	82341	Iron Screw	69 gross	66.2 × 17.40 × 7.70	20hp 2-cyl.	J. & J. Hay
1881	Leo	84346	Iron Screw	51 gross	65.6 × 15.90 × 6.10	18hp 1-cyl.	J. & J. Hay
1881	Delta	85882	Iron Screw	68 gross	65.6 × 17.50 × 7.50	25hp 2-cyl.	J. & J. Hay
1884	*Dinah	93387	Iron Screw	53 gross	66.5 × 17.20 × 6.70	25hp 2-cyl.	J. & J. Hay
1884	*(Craigielea)	98635	Iron Screw	67 gross	67.0 × 17.20 × 6.40	12hp 2-cyl.	J. & J. Hay
1886	*Amy	99793	Iron Screw	43 gross	66.0 × 16.20 × 5.20	10hp 1-cyl.	J. & J. Hay
1886	Albert (2)	93326	Iron Screw	53 gross	66.0 × 16.40 × 6.20	16hp 1-cyl.	J. & J. Hay
1887	Scotia (2)	93375	Iron Screw	56 gross	66.0 × 16.40 × 6.40	25hp 1-cyl.	J. & J. Hay
1888	Beatrice	106029	Iron Screw	39 gross	66.0 × 13.20 × 5.60	15hp 2-cyl.	J. & J. Hay
1888	Alice (2)	106044	Iron Screw	44 gross	66.0 × 13.20 × 5.20	15hp 2-cyl.	J. & J. Hay
1889	Aniline		Iron Screw				J. Ross & Co., Falkirk
1890	Orion	98581	Iron Screw	79 gross	66.0 × 18.00 × 7.50	13hp 2-cyl.	J. & J. Hay
1892	Argo	98692	Iron Screw	61 gross	65.5 × 16.00 × 6.90	25hp 2-cyl.	J. & J. Hay
1892	Neptune	99851	Iron Screw	80 gross	66.0 × 18.10 × 8.25	20hp 2-cyl.	J. & J. Hay
1893	Nelson	102586	Iron Screw	81 gross	66.0 × 18.10 × 6.25	20hp 2-cyl.	J. & J. Hay

Year	Name	O.N.	Type	Tons	Dimensions	Engine	Owner
1893	*Briton*	102655	Iron Screw	83 gross	65.8 × 18.00 × 8.40	17hp 2-cyl.	J. & J. Hay
1894	*Celt*	104530	Iron Screw	58 gross	66.0 × 16.20 × 6.50	25hp 2-cyl.	J. & J. Hay
1894	*Saxon*	104583	Iron Screw	85 gross	65.8 × 18.00 × 8.40	17hp 2-cyl.	J. & J. Hay
1895	*Vulcan*	104641	Iron Screw	44 gross	66.0 × 16.30 × 5.30	16hp 2-cyl.	J. & J. Hay
1895	*Norman*	105951	Iron Screw	85 gross	65.8 × 18.00 × 8.40	17hp 2-cyl.	J. & J. Hay
1896	*Hero*	106028	Iron Screw	44 gross	66.0 × 16.30 × 5.30	15hp 2-cyl.	J. & J. Hay
1896	*Briton* (2)	106023	Steel Screw	85 gross	65.8 × 18.00 × 8.40	17hp 2-cyl.	J. & J. Hay

J. & J. HAY LTD.

Year	Name	O.N.	Type	Tons	Dimensions	Engine	Owner
1896	*Victor*	106042	Iron Screw	44 gross	66.0 × 16.30 × 5.30	15hp 2-cyl.	J. & J. Hay Ltd.
1897	*Gael*	106087	Steel Screw	85 gross	65.8 × 18.00 × 8.40	17hp 2-cyl.	J. & J. Hay Ltd.
1897	*Tartar*	108693	Steel Screw	89 gross	66.0 × 18.00 × 8.60	17hp 2-cyl.	J. & J. Hay Ltd.
1898	*Dane*	108752	Steel Screw	69 gross	66.0 × 16.85 × 7.05	25hp 2-cyl.	J. & J. Hay Ltd.
1899	*Druid*	111218	Steel Screw	92 gross	66.0 × 18.00 × 8.60	17hp 2-cyl.	J. & J. Hay Ltd.
1900	*Turk*	111297	Steel Screw	65 gross	66.35 × 16.75 × 6.75	15hp 2-cyl.	J. & J. Hay Ltd.
1901	*Moor*	113954	Steel Screw	89 gross	66.0 × 18.05 × 8.70	17hp 2-cyl.	J. & J. Hay Ltd.
1902	*Greek*	136300	Steel Screw	64 gross	66.3 × 16.85 × 6.85	15hp 2-cyl.	J. & J. Hay Ltd.
1902			2 Iron Scows				J. & J. Hay Ltd.
1903	*Dane* (2) renamed *Saxon* (3)	136271	Steel Screw	64 gross	66.0 × 16.80 × 6.85	15hp 2-cyl.	J. & J. Hay Ltd.
1904	*Roman*	133150	Steel Screw	69 gross	66.4 × 17.20 × 6.90	12hp 2-cyl.	J. & J. Hay Ltd.
1904	*Saxon* (2) renamed *Gascon*	133008	Steel Screw	64 gross	66.3 × 17.20 × 6.80	18hp 2-cyl.	J. & J. Hay Ltd.
1905	*Briton* (4)	121221	Steel Screw	68 gross	66.3 × 17.95 × 8.50	17hp 2-cyl.	J. & J. Hay Ltd.
1905	*Trojan*	121256	Steel Screw	65 gross	66.6 × 17.20 × 6.80	15hp 2-cyl.	J. & J. Hay Ltd.
1905	*Druid* (2)	121286	Steel Screw	68 gross	66.5 × 17.95 × 8.55	17hp 2-cyl.	J. & J. Hay Ltd.
1907	*Celt* (2)	124183	Steel Screw	69 gross	66.3 × 17.25 × 6.80	15hp 2-cyl.	J. & J. Hay Ltd.
1908	*Cossack*	124250	Steel Screw	92 gross	66.3 × 18.10 × 8.80	17hp 2-cyl.	J. & J. Hay Ltd.
1910	*Cretan*	129474	Steel Screw	92 Gross	66.0 × 18.00 × 8.60	17hp 2-cyl.	J. & J. Hay Ltd.
1916	*Serb*	137817	Steel Screw	93 gross	66.65 × 18.00 × 8.80	17hp 2-cyl.	J. & J. Hay Ltd.

Year	Name	O.N.	Type	Tons	Dimensions	Engine	Owner
				J. HAY & SONS LTD.			
1925	*Moor* (2)	147898	Steel Screw	97 gross	66.0 × 18.35 × 8.65	18hp 2-cyl.	J. Hay & Sons Ltd.
1927	*Serb* (2)	160186	Steel Screw	95 gross	66.0 × 18.35 × 8.65	18hp 2-cyl.	J. Hay & Sons Ltd.
1929	*Turk* (2)	160240	Steel Screw	70 gross	65.4 × 17.10 × 6.65	75ihp 2-cyl.	J. Hay & Sons Ltd.
1931	*Gael* (2)	161941	Steel Screw	70 gross	65.3 × 17.60 × 6.70	75ihp 2-cyl.	J. Hay & Sons Ltd.
1932	*Slav*	161965	Steel Screw	68 gross	65.5 × 17.60 × 6.70	75ihp 2-cyl.	J. Hay & Sons Ltd.
1934	*Tuscan*	164043	Steel Screw	93 gross	66.0 × 18.35 × 8.65	18hp 2-cyl.	J. Hay & Sons Ltd.
1935	*Cuban*	164065	Steel Screw	72 gross	65.6 × 17.55 × 6.80	70ihp 2-cyl.	J. Hay & Sons Ltd.
1937	*Texan*	164106	Steel Screw	71 gross	66.4 × 17.55 × 6.85	52nhp 2-cyl.	J. Hay & Sons Ltd.
1938	*Inca*	165958	Steel Screw	72 gross	66.4 × 17.55 × 6.85	60ehp 2-cyl.	J. Hay & Sons Ltd.
1939	*Cretan* (2)	165972	Steel Screw	72 gross	66.4 × 17.55 × 6.85	60ehp 2-cyl.	J. Hay & Sons Ltd.
1941	*Boer*	168673	Steel Screw	72 gross	66.4 × 17.55 × 6.85	60ehp 2-cyl.	J. Hay & Sons Ltd.
1942	*Vic* 18 renamed *Spartan* (3)	168712	Steel Screw	99 gross	66.75 × 18.50 × 8.80	17hp 2-cyl.	H.M. the King.
1944	*Kaffir*	169405	Steel Screw	99 gross	66.75 × 18.50 × 8.80	17hp 2-cyl.	J. Hay & Sons Ltd.
1945	*Chindit*	169456	Steel Screw	74 gross	67.1 × 17.55 × 6.80	50ihp 2-cyl.	J. Hay & Sons Ltd.

* Of the four vessels marked with an asterisk, *Ceres* is said to have been launched as a dumb lighter; *Dinah*, *Craigielea* and *Amy* were launched as dumb lighters.

There is an unsubstantiated tradition that *Ceres* was built at Kirkintilloch as an iron dumb lighter in 1865. *Dinah*, launched as a dumb lighter in 1884, was converted to steam in 1887. *Craigielea* was launched as a dumb lighter in 1884. It is uncertain whether she had a name at that time. If she had, it is unlikely to have been *Craigielea*. She was engined in 1891, when she went to J. Glover of Paisley. It is probable that she was given the name *Craigielea* at that time, when she was registered. *Amy* was launched as a dumb lighter in 1886 and converted to steam in 1889.

VESSELS BUILT AT CANAL BASIN YARD

Year	Name	O.N.	Type	Tons	Dimensions	Engine	Owner
				P. McGREGOR & SONS			
1874	*Laburnum*	71690	Wooden Ketch	54 gross	65.5 × 18.60 × 7.20		P. McGregor, Kirkintilloch
1902	*Scout*	115714	Steel Screw	97 gross	66.2 × 18.15 × 8.80	25hp 1-cyl.	Coasting Steamships
1902	*Sentry*	115745	Steel Screw	96 gross	66.1 × 18.15 × 8.80	25hp 1-cyl.	Coasting Steamships
1903	*Oriental*		Iron Screw	70 gross		225ihp	Foreign

Year	Name	O.N.	Type	Tons	Dimensions	Engine	Owner
1903	*May Queen*	115772	Steel Screw	56 gross	67.2×15.15×7.00	22nhp 2-cyl.	J. Aitken, Kirkintilloch
1903	*Sentinel*	115784	Steel Screw	95 gross	67.0×18.35×8.80	17hp 1-cyl.	Coasting Steamships
1903	*Sergeant*	119068	Steel Screw	95 gross	66.8×18.35×8.75	17hp 1-cyl.	Coasting Steamships
1903	*Active*	117533	Steel Screw Tug	38 gross	59.4×14.00×6.10	20rhp 2-cyl.	Yare & Waveney, Yarmouth
1904	*Proyda*	119112	Steel Screw Tug	56 gross	66.0×16.50×6.80	50nhp 2-cyl.	Russian Owner, Odessa
1904	*No. 19*		Steel Screw Tug	70 gross		200ihp	
1904	*Cuca*		Steel Screw	99 gross		150ihp	Foreign
1904	*Commercio Bermeano*		Steel Screw	99 gross		150ihp	Foreign
1905	*Merlin*		Iron Screw	151 gross			
1905	*Normand*		Steel Screw	269 gross			
1905	*Provencal* 15	70756	Steel Screw	53 gross	68.0×16.40×6.50	50nhp 2-cyl.	Soc. Anon. Provencale de Remorquage, Marseille
1905	*Margaret*	121233	Steel Screw	54 gross	66.0×15.85×7.6	25hp 1-cyl.	W. E. Colebrooke, Rye
1905	*No. 15*		Iron Screw	25 gross		100ihp	
1905	*No. 16*		Iron Screw	30 gross		100ihp	
1905	*No. 18*		Iron Screw	30 gross		120ihp	
1906	*Mars*	121339	Steel Screw Tug	47 gross	69.0×15.10×8.05	40nhp 2-cyl.	W. Isaacs, Liverpool
1906	*Pioneer*	123242	Steel Screw Tug	50 gross	69.0×15.10×8.05	40rhp 2-cyl.	W. Gillyott, Hull
1906	*No. 27*		Steel Screw	85 gross			Foreign
1906	*No. 28*		Steel Screw	55 gross			Foreign
1907	*Beaumont*	124160	Steel Screw Tug	58 gross	69.0×16.6×8.50	60rhp 2-cyl.	Stewart & Fulton, Glasgow
1907	*Rayo*		Steel Screw Tug	35 gross	59.6×14.70×6.60	24hp 2-cyl.	R. Orchard, Antofagasta, Chile
1907	*Rosario*		Steel Screw	22 gross	50.0×12.60×5.50	14hp 2-cyl.	Wilson & Son, Bahia, Brazil
1907	*Manati*		Steel Screw Tug	58 gross	68.9×15.10×6.10	49nhp 2-cyl.	Booth S.S. Co., Manaos, Brazil
1907	*Darfeel*		Steel Screw Tug	60 gross		300ihp	Egyptian
1907	*No. 29*		Steel Screw	45 gross		120ihp	Foreign
1907	*No. 30*		Steel Barge	104 gross			Foreign
1908	*Teyr-el-Behr*		Steel Screw Tug	64 gross	72.0×16.50×8.90	300ihp 2-cyl.	Egyptian Coastguard
1908	*No. 25*		Steel Screw Tug	48 gross		250ihp	

81

Year	Name	O.N.	Type	Tons	Dimensions	Engine	Owner
1908	*No. 26*	124261	Steel Screw Tug	49 gross	$69.0 \times 15.10 \times 8.10$	28nhp 2-cyl.	Stewart & Fulton, Glasgow
1908	*Suramento*		Launch	10 gross		50ihp	Foreign
1908	*No. 35*		Steel Screw Tug	31 gross		150ihp	Foreign
1908	*No. 37*		Steel TS Tug	55 gross		300ihp	Colonial
1908	*No. 40*		Steel Barge	25 gross			Colonial
1908	*Eider*		Steel Screw Tug	31 gross	$54.0 \times 13.30 \times 5.80$	150ihp 2-cyl.	E.I. Distilleries, Madras
1909	*No. 44*		Steel Screw	60 gross		350ihp	
1909	*Kent Colebrooke*		Steel Screw	52 gross		150ihp	
1909	*Rosyth* No. 1	71657	Steel Screw	26 gross	$55.2 \times 13.10 \times 5.80$	19rhp 2-cyl.	Admiralty
1909	*Beauview*	128252	Steel Screw Tug	49 gross	$68.8 \times 15.10 \times 8.10$	32rhp 2-cyl.	Stewart & Fulton, Glasgow
1909	*Maya*		Launch	15 gross		60ihp	
1909	*Endrick*		Motor Launch	3 gross		20ihp	
1910	*Ardfern*	129527	Steel Screw	99 gross	$66.5 \times 18.35 \times 9.30$	26hp 2-cyl	Dougall & Stirrat, Glasgow
1910	*No. 47*		Steel Screw	80 gross		450ihp	
1910	*No. 48*		Steel Screw	80 gross		450ihp	
1910	*No. 49*		Steel Scow	27 gross			Foreign
1911	*Torias*		Steel Screw	70 gross			French Owner
1911	*No. 50*		Steel Screw	85 gross		350ihp	Colonial
1911	*No. 51*		Wooden ML	5 gross		50ihp	Colonial
1911	*No. 52*		Steel ML	30 gross		180ihp	Colonial
1912	*North Star*		Steel Screw Tug	35 gross	$55.4 \times 13.00 \times 6.40$	140ihp 2-cyl.	North Russian Trading Company
1912	*No. 45*	133052	Steel Screw	32 gross	$55.4 \times 13.00 \times 6.40$	17hp 1-cyl.	A. McDougall, Glasgow.
1912	*Innisagra*	133047	Steel Screw MV	94 gross	$65.6 \times 18.40 \times 8.70$	80bhp 2-cyl.	Coasting Motor Shipping Co.
1912	*Innisbeg*	133064	Steel Screw MV	94 gross	$65.65 \times 18.40 \times 8.70$	80nhp 2-cyl.	Coasting Motor Shipping Co.
1912	*Inniscroone* renamed *Truro Trader*	133061	Steel Screw MV	94 gross	$65.65 \times 18.40 \times 8.70$	80bhp 2-cyl.	Coasting Motor Shipping Co.
1912	*Innisdhu* renamed *Ben Olliver*	133086	Steel Screw MV	94 gross	$65.65 \times 18.40 \times 8.70$	100bhp 2-cyl.	Coasting Motor Shipping Co.
1913	*Inniseane*	133108	Steel Screw MV	94 gross	$65.95 \times 18.40 \times 8.70$	110ihp 2-cyl.	Coasting Motor Shipping co.
1913	*Innisfree*	133115	Steel Screw MV	94 gross	$65.9 \times 18.40 \times 8.70$	110ihp 2-cyl.	Coasting Motor Shipping Co.

Year	Name	O.N.	Type	Tons	Dimensions	Engine	Owner
1913	*Innisclora*	133146	Steel Screw MV	117 reg	74.7×18.30×8.70	26nhp 2-cyl.	Coasting Motor Shipping Co.
1913	*Innishowen* renamed *Eva Petersen*	133156	Steel Screw MV	118 reg	74.1×18.30×8.70	26nhp 2-cyl.	Coasting Motor Shipping Co.
1912	*No. 65*		Steel Barge	10 gross			
1912	*No. 66*		Steel Barge	10 gross			
1913	*No. 69*		Steel Screw Tug	53 gross		150ihp	
1914	*Sir Walter Raine*		Steel TS		47.0×14.50×4.50		Sunderland Corporation
1914	*Draig Goch*	58382	Steel Screw Tug	43 gross	69.0×16.00×6.80	26rhp 2-cyl.	Portmadoc Towage Co.
1915	*Thegon*	129319	Steel TS	174 gross	110.5×21.60×10.5	44rhp 4-cyl.	Petroleum S.S. Co.
1916	*Perfection*	137821	Steel Screw MV	73 gross	64.0×17.55×7.10	I.C. 2 str.	Anglo-American Oil Co.
1920	*Buckie Burn*	55396	Steel Screw	51 gross	69.0×16.10×7.70	26rhp 2-cyl.	Admiralty
1920	*Rathven Burn*	69855	Steel Screw	51 gross	69.0×16.10×7.70	27nhp 2-cyl.	Admiralty
1920	*Benfinch*	54514	Steel Screw	113 gross	75.3×18.60×8.90	30rhp 2-cyl.	E. H. Bennet & Co., Newport, Mon.
1920	*Kenfinch*	64148	Steel Screw	113 gross	75.3×18.60×8.90	30rhp 2-cyl.	E. H. Bennett & Co., Newport, Mon.
1921	*Rockfinch*	71488	Steel Screw	114 gross	75.3×18.60×9.90	13nhp 2-cyl.	E. H. Bennett & Co., Newport, Mon.
1921	*Starfinch*	73873	Steel Screw	114 gross	75.2×18.60×8.90	30rhp 2-cyl.	E. H. Bennett & Co., Newport, Mon.
1921	*Wynor*	144254	Steel Screw	113 gross	75.3×18.60×8.90	13nhp 2-cyl.	J. Stewart, Glasgow

NOTE:—When a number is given in place of a name in the name column, it is the vessel's yard number. It indicates that the vessel had not been given a name at the time of compilation of the list in which the number appeared.

This list is not a complete list of building at the yard, but includes as many vessels as have been traced by the writer.